Immigrant and Native Workers

Contrasts and Competition

Thomas R. Bailey

WESTVIEW PRESS
BOULDER AND LONDON

Conservation of Human Resources Studies in the New Economy

Published in 1987 in the United States of America by Westview Press, Inc.; Frederick A. Praeger, Publisher; 5500 Central Avenue, Boulder, Colorado 80301

Library of Congress Cataloging-in-Publication Data
Bailey, Thomas Raymond.
    Immigrant and native workers.
    (Conservation of Human Resources studies in the
new economy)
    Includes bibliographies and index.
    1. Alien labor—United States. 2. Minorities—
Employment—United States. I. Title. II. Series.
HD8081.A5B35 1987 331.6'2'0973 86-28205
ISBN 0-8133-7349-2

Printed and bound in the United States of America

The paper used in this publication meets the requirements of the American National Standard for Permanence of Paper for Printed Library Materials Z39.48-1984.

6   5   4   3   2   1

For Carmenza

Contents

Tables

Foreword

As chair of federal employment and training commissions for twenty years, I presided at only one meeting that was out of control from beginning to end: a meeting to explore changes in U.S. immigration policy affecting the temporary admission of foreign workers into the country. What I learned that day was that "immigration and employment" issues are unlike many other issues in the public arena: They elicit intensely charged emotional and intellectual attitudes, arguments, and advice.

In this book, Dr. Thomas R. Bailey deals with issues in this contentious arena: What is the impact of both legal and illegal immigrants on the labor market experiences of vulnerable native groups, such as youth, women, and black men, who look for jobs in the same restaurant, clothing, and construction industries in which many immigrants seek to make their way?

The outstanding contribution of Bailey's work is its disciplined approach in which emotions and generalizations are muted in favor of sophisticated analysis, the skillful use of empirical data, and focused case studies. In an arena in which strong views often crowd out careful analysis, Bailey stresses the latter and disregards the former. He provides a penetrating analysis of how immigrants and native workers with limited skills find jobs and advance occupationally. What can be learned from this analysis?

- In order to understand the interaction between the various low-skilled groups in this labor market, it is essential to look beyond their shared skill level and examine the goals and motivations that bring them to the labor market and the processes and mechanisms through which they find jobs and learn skills.
- The immigration process shapes the employment of the newcomers in ways that differentiate their labor market roles from those of low-skilled natives.

- Networking is crucial for most immigrants. They seek work where others have found employment and with employers from their own ethnic groups.
- Ethnic enclaves provide on-the-job training for many of the newcomers. Eventually, many immigrants are able to acquire the managerial skills and knowledge that enable them to start their own businesses.
- An in-depth analysis of the restaurant industry demonstrates how forms of ownership, uses of technology, and specialization of jobs lead to different patterns of employee recruitment and training.
- This differentiation of types of workers and types of jobs mitigates the competition between immigrants and unskilled natives. At most, a reduction in the inflow of immigrants might have some positive effects on the labor market experience of native women.
- In the construction industry, there are differences between the job opportunities open to black men and to recent immigrants. Black men are more likely to obtain jobs in the unionized sector because of affirmative action programs, whereas immigrants are more likely to be hired by friends or relatives who own small, nonunionized firms that focus on the rehabilitation of residential properties.
- The presumption that the illegal status of undocumented workers has a major influence on their labor market roles and impact is not substantiated. In fact, their behavior in the urban labor market is not readily distinguishable from immigrants who work in the United States legally.

There are many other interesting and significant findings in Bailey's book, but the work as a whole is more important than its several parts. His book advances our understanding of the dynamics of the urban labor market as it affects individuals who have limited skills and are handicapped in the labor market by their race, gender, and age. The book also provides a framework for sorting out the relative advantages and disadvantages encountered by immigrants as they gain skills and competences. Bailey's most important lesson is that one must not rely on extant theories to explore and illuminate the complexities of the urban labor scene. Rather, one must seek to improve on these theories by organizing data that reflect the true complexities of the urban labor market. Further cross-sectional analysis will not suffice. People live on a temporal trajectory and their present jobs are often training stations for their next jobs. Both the dynamics and the details of the market must be studied and understood. Bailey has set a high standard for research scholars to follow in their work on urban labor markets. That is his most important and lasting contribution in this book.

Eli Ginzberg
Director,
Conservation of Human Resources,
Columbia University

Acknowledgments

Many friends and colleagues deserve thanks for their help in carrying out this research and preparing the book. Without the encouragement of Eli Ginzberg, the research would never have been completed. As the director of Conservation of Human Resources, he has established a flexible, supportive, and intellectually stimulating work environment. Marcia Freedman spent many hours discussing my research and reading the drafts. Many of the ideas and insights developed in the book had their origins in conversations with her. Michael Piore initially kindled my interest in labor markets in general and in immigrants in particular. His work has served as both an inspiration and a guide to my own research. Over the past five years, Roger Waldinger and I have engaged in an extensive dialogue on these issues and his influence has inevitably found its way into my work. And through my almost daily conversations with Thierry Noyelle, I have learned a great deal not only about labor markets and employment but also about how to organize and present ideas. Josh DeWind, Harry Katz, Paul Osterman, David Reimers, and Peter Temin also read drafts and gave many suggestions and criticisms.

This research was started with a grant from the Charles H. Revson Foundation. Over the course of the project, financial support was also provided by the Rockefeller Foundation and the Alfred P. Sloan Foundation.

Charles Frederick was of much appreciated assistance in practical matters. Penny Peace edited the book and helped both to improve the writing and to ease the process of preparing the manuscript. Ellen Levine, Shoshana Vasheetz, and Fedor Kabalin typed the many drafts. Research assistance was provided at various times during the project by Charlene Blount, Joanne Kohler, Robert Montei, Michael Pagnam, Amy Waldman, and Sarah Bingman.

My wife, Carmenza, not only provided constant encouragement and emotional support but contributed much more. We discussed every chapter many times and I could not have done without her criticism and insight. Furthermore, she conducted some of the interviews with restaurant owners and she shared with me her own research on immigrant employment in the construction industry.   Finally, I particularly want to thank my two daughters, Erika and Daniela, for helping me to keep my perspective throughout the process of research and writing.

Thomas R. Bailey

1

Introduction:
Beyond Low Skills

The enactment of the Immigration Reform and Control Act of 1986 culminated over a decade of efforts to reorganize the nation's immigration system. Although the annual flow of immigrants may be reduced under the law, the combination of its provisions and the resources that will be available for enforcement will still permit the arrival of several hundred thousand newcomers every year. We will, therefore, have a continuing need to understand the nature of the economic and social impact of immigration in order to evaluate and plan future reforms and annual enforcement budgets and strategies.

The role that immigrants play in the labor market has been a central problem throughout the years of discussion and debate. This book focuses on the impact of immigration on the employment of three groups of natives with whom immigrants[1] are presumed to compete: teenagers, women, and black men. Given the controversy surrounding the labor market effects of immigration, it is surprising that there is still only a handful of studies that focus on the issue. Moreover, most of the research that is available does not differentiate among the effects of immigration on particular native groups. Research on immigration's impact on the employment of youth and women is particularly scarce.

But the goals of the analysis go beyond a quantitative measurement of the employment effects. Indeed, a primary purpose of the research is to develop a more concrete understanding of how immigrants and natives interact in the labor market. Most analyses devote little attention to the actual interaction; rather, analysts rely on the simplistic assumption that most of the newcomers have few skills and therefore compete with natives for jobs at the bottom of the employment hierarchy. This focus on low skills and the implicit model within which it is used creates a powerful theoretical argument that immigration weakens the employment position of low-skilled natives. Nevertheless, the research that is available simply does not reveal strong displacement effects.

One reason for the apparent inconsistency is that the analytic focus on skill levels is misleading. This book uses a set of industry case studies in conjunction with analyses of aggregate data to argue that factors other than skill levels differentiate the roles of immigrant and native workers. These differences are not so much in the skills themselves but in the expectations and goals that group members bring to their jobs and in the mechanisms and processes through which they enter the labor market, acquire skills, and achieve or fail to achieve occupational mobility. For the foreign born, these factors emerge directly from the economic and social transition inherent in the process of immigration. That process itself shapes immigrant labor force participation in ways that differentiate it from the participation of low-skilled natives. Moreover, the case studies reveal that these contrasts in labor market roles mitigate the competition between the groups, a conclusion that is consistent with analyses of aggregate data that find at most weak negative employment or wage effects.

The study, therefore, approaches the issue of the labor market impact of immigration from a new perspective. In contrast to the few existing empirical studies that are based at least implicitly on the assumption that unskilled native and immigrant workers are substitutes, the approach taken here identifies the similarities and dissimilarities between the roles of these groups, elaborates on the main causes of the differences between them, describes how the differences interact with the economy, and draws out the implications for labor market competition. Thus the book not only provides a greater understanding of the extent of competition and how that competition comes about, but it also strengthens the conceptual and theoretical basis for empirical measurement of the interactions between these groups.

Moreover, the implications of the argument go beyond competition between immigrants and natives. Although there is much historical, descriptive, and quantitative research on teenagers, women, minorities, and other groups with subordinate roles in the economy, most of this research is aimed primarily at understanding why each of these groups differs from adult white males. In contrast, this analysis focuses on interactions among the subordinate groups. Thus, finally, the book is a study of the low-wage labor market and the interactions among the workers who fill many of its jobs.

Skill Levels and the Labor Market Role
of Immigrants

Understanding the impact of immigration depends fundamentally on conceptions of the relevant characteristics of immigrant and native workers and how these characteristics interact with the structure of the receiving economy. The importance of the underlying model can be made clear by asking why immigrants are expected to have any labor market effect at all. Immigration is a form of population increase, yet there is no a priori reason to believe that employment and labor markets will differ in two countries with different-sized populations. But immigration can have an effect because the relevant characteristics such as wealth, skills, and age are not the same in the foreign-born as in the native-born population. The assumptions underlying the analyses are rarely explicitly examined, but the discussion of the labor market impact is usually based on two assumptions about the characteristics of immigrants: Immigrants have little capital and few skills.

If immigrants have no capital, then, at least in the short run, their arrival will not increase the resources or the number of machines with which the labor force works. More workers with the same amount of capital will probably lead to lower productivity per worker and, consequently, lower wages and employment for native workers.

But even more than the assumed lack of wealth, in discussing the consequences of immigration, social scientists, policymakers, and the public have focused on the low skill levels of the foreign born. Indeed this is seen as the fundamental determinant of their labor market role and impact and is the assumption on which both formal models and more general discussions have been based. For example, former Undersecretary of Labor Malcolm Lovell, testifying in favor of immigration restriction, argued that immigrants, especially illegal immigrants, typically find employment in "low-skilled industrial, service and farm jobs."[2] Vernon Briggs has argued that the foreign born in all categories—resident aliens, refugees, nonimmigrant workers, and illegals—are not only concentrated among the unskilled, but that these groups also are increasingly composed of less-skilled individuals.[3] Michael Piore has also emphasized the immigrant role in filling low-skilled, low-quality jobs.[4]

Formal economic models of the labor market effects of immigration invariably include newcomers among the unskilled.[5] The economists who develop these models assume that skilled and unskilled labor work with machines or physical capital to produce output and that immigrants are perfect substitutes for unskilled native workers. The models imply that the labor market position of unskilled natives deteriorates as a result of immigration while benefits accrue to skilled workers and to owners of capital.[6] Thus, in both the formal models and the less formal discussions, it is the concentration of immigrants among the unskilled that results in lower wages and higher unemployment at the lower levels of the employment hierarchy.

One problem with the emphasis on low skill levels is that many immigrants arrive with skills. Indeed, foreign-born newcomers are more diverse than popular conceptions suggest. Immigrants to the United States do not come from the poorest segments of their native societies. Nor are they all unskilled; foreign-born individuals enumerated by the 1980 census who arrived in the United States between 1975 and 1980 had on average almost twelve years of schooling.[7]

Nevertheless, it is true that immigrants are concentrated in low-skill and low-wage positions either because they arrive with few skills or because the skills with which they arrive are of limited use in this economy.[8] The occupational distribution of immigrants also demonstrates that they are concentrated at the lower levels of the employment hierarchy. For example, in New York City in 1980, the foreign born were underrepresented in managerial, professional, and administrative support positions and overrepresented among service workers and operatives.[9]

Despite their concentration at the low end of the labor market and the plausibility of the simple argument that large numbers of unskilled immigrants compete directly with groups of disadvantaged native-born workers, the argument does not appear to be consistent with many developments in the labor market. There is no obvious relationship between labor market distress among various native groups and the presence of immigrants. For example, unemployment rates in 1984 for all blacks, black teenagers, and all teenagers in California, Florida, and Texas (states with large immigrant populations) were below the national rates for these groups.[10] In New York State, black teenage unemployment was above the national average, but black adults had a lower than average unemployment rate. And to use a more narrowly focused example drawn from a later chapter, although immigrants are significantly overrepresented in the restaurant industry in New York City and despite the dramatic growth of the city's immigrant population during the 1970s, the teenage share of the industry's employment increased sharply between 1970 and 1980.

These are simple examples, but more complicated empirical research has failed to reveal strong displacement. The studies usually compare wage or unemployment levels of particular groups of natives in Standard Metropolitan Statistical Areas (SMSAs) with large immigrant populations to those levels in SMSAs with few foreign-born workers. Some studies have concluded that there are moderate negative labor market effects for some natives.[11] Other studies have found no relationship between the presence of immigrants and the labor market position of various native groups. And still others have found evidence that the presence of immigrants strengthens the employment position of some native groups that tend to work for low wages.[12] All of these studies have methodological weaknesses,[13] but given the general theoretical consensus on the competition between immigrants and unskilled workers, it is surprising that a firm empirical relationship is not more easily established.

Contrasts Between Low-Skilled Immigrants and Natives

In contrast to the implicit assumption that unskilled immigrant and native workers are perfect substitutes, the case studies reported in this book show that they play very different roles in the industries examined. Thus, it is not surprising that a conceptual framework focused on skill levels that recognizes no differences between these groups is of limited use in analyzing the interactions between them.[14] A central goal of this book is to develop a better understanding of the similarities and contrasts between immigrants and natives with few skills. This section outlines the central factors that set these groups apart from each other.

Workers do not bring their skills to the labor market in a vacuum. Not only do attitudes, expectations, and cultural backgrounds influence labor market behavior, but employment also competes with other activities and interests and takes place within an institutional and legal context, the implications of which are not the same for every individual. For example, teenagers, women with small children, middle-aged men who have lost assembly-line jobs, actors looking for part-time work, and immigrants hoping to save enough money to buy a business in their home countries may all be equally unskilled, but they are not all appropriate for the same jobs.

One key to differentiating the labor market roles of immigrants from those of low-skilled natives is the influence of the immigration process itself. Immigrants of all ethnic and cultural backgrounds have in common a transitional experience that is not shared with the native born. Immigrants are in the process of moving from one culture to another and between economies with large differences in standards of living, and almost all immigrants, at least for a time, are ambivalent in their commitment to those two societies. It is the expectations and attitudes that emerge from the partial and shifting attachments to two societies, cultures, and economies and the particular pattern of opportunities and labor market barriers they face that separate the newcomers from the incumbents.

One distinction between immigrants and natives that has been discussed in the research on competition concerns the former's lingering attachment to and identification with their home countries. This argument, which was developed by Michael Piore, suggests that immigrants regard their commitment to the U.S. labor market as temporary and purely instrumental—a means to earn money for remittances or purchases back home.[15] Indeed, Piore argued that most immigrants initially do not plan to stay permanently in the United States. Due to this perspective, immigrants are willing to take jobs that, because of their low wages and low status, are unacceptable to natives. Linking this difference to the basic assumptions of the segmented labor market model, Piore suggested that competition between the two groups is not a serious problem. Immigrants are recruited by employers for secondary-sector jobs that natives reject, and the segmentation of the labor market prevents the influx of immigrants from affecting the jobs in other sectors where natives are employed.[16] Furthermore, to the extent that the two sectors are complementary, immigration actually improves the labor market positions of native workers by strengthening the secondary sector. Indeed, this view of the role of immigrants is frequently cited by opponents of greater immigration restriction.

But this focus on a willingness to work in low-quality jobs and a short-term perspective on employment in the United States is not adequate to differentiate immigrants from many low-skilled natives. Immigrants are not alone in the secondary sector. It is their employment in the secondary sector that, according to segmented labor market theory, explains why the earnings of many minorities and women are lower than those of white males even after accounting for differences in age and education. If it is their temporary and contingent commitment to the U.S. labor market that defines the labor market role of immigrants, many native teenagers, adult women, and others share such a perspective. Thus, although the segmented labor market concept suggests that competition between immigrants and adult males or primary-sector workers is weak, it implies that immigrants and other groups that historically have filled secondary-sector jobs are indeed thrown together in the same low-wage labor markets.[17]

Whereas the immigrants' orientation to their home countries and their plans to return are one explanation of why immigrants do not compete with primary-sector workers, the argument in this book puts more emphasis on the actual processes and mechanisms through which immigrants adjust to the receiving country. Although it is through these processes that immigrants, or more frequently their children, become more like natives, the process itself does differentiate immigrants from native secondary-sector workers—teenagers and many women and minorities.

The importance of focusing on the dynamic nature of the immigration process becomes clear when considering immigrant skill levels. It may be true that newcomers arrive with few marketable skills, but they do not remain unskilled. Through their subsequent employment experience and sometimes through formal education they acquire skills that allow them to move up through the occupational hierarchy and increase their earnings. And the immigration process creates important distinctions between the ways that immigrants and natives learn skills and achieve occupational mobility. In this regard, it is interesting that the image of the industrious immigrant who fulfills the American dream is more firmly established than that of the exploited immigrant who is a threat to low-skilled natives.

There is already a large body of research on the process of immigration to the United States. The settlement and adjustment of turn-of-the-century and early twentieth-century immigrants from Europe and Asia have been chronicled in countless books and articles, and the apparent success of these immigrants has spawned controversy about why native blacks have experienced less mobility.[18] The progress of more recent immigrants has also been scrutinized by many analysts.[19] Research so far has suggested that within twenty years after immigration, the earnings of immigrants appear to equal those of natives of the same age, sex, race, and educational background.[20]

Efforts to understand the economic and social adaptation of immigrants have also led to an examination of immigrant self-employment. Almost all foreign-born groups are overrepresented among small business owners and the research in this area generally concludes that entrepreneurship has played an important role in the economic adjustment of many immigrants.[21] An important outgrowth of this research has been a broader analysis of the role of ethnic businesses and immigrant economic enclaves in the economic mobility of workers as well as owners. It was first argued by Kenneth Wilson and Alejandro Portes that there appeared to be advantages for Cuban workers employed in Cuban-owned firms.[22] Other studies have since explored the benefits derived by employees working for coethnics.[23]

Despite abundant research on immigrant economic mobility and adaptation, the insights developed by many of these studies have never been integrated into analyses of the impact of immigration. Most research on immigrant adaptation has focused precisely on the transitions involved both in the movement from one country to another and on the adjustments in the postimmigration period. But discussion and research on the impact of immigration continue to be based on a static view of immigrants as unskilled workers. Thus, one of the goals of this book is to merge these two streams of research and to consider the labor market implications of the dynamic aspects of the immigration process.

The analysis developed in this book has policy implications in several areas. A better understanding of the impact and labor market role of immigration will be useful in designing national immigration policy; but just as important, the institutional and process-oriented approach used here can help local and state policymakers to cope with the problems associated with the arrival of large numbers of immigrants. Municipal and state governments have no control over the number of immigrants in their labor markets. For them, an immigration policy must directly confront the problems associated with immigration. To do this, governments can encourage particular types of business development, promote investment in target neighborhoods, design training or remediation specifically for groups affected by immigration or for immigrants themselves, or adjust eligibility requirements for income support programs. Aggregate estimates of the degree of competition between immigrants and natives can, in isolation, provide little guidance for this type of policy. Because the analysis focuses on the mechanisms and processes of skill acquisition, the book also has implications for education policy and for measures designed to facilitate the economic mobility of natives as well as of immigrants.

Methodology and Scope

The book's analysis is primarily based on case studies of the employment of immigrants in particular industries. The studies rely on information gathered in interviews with employers, supplemented by public data and secondary sources. The case study approach is particularly useful for comparing and contrasting the roles of each group of workers within the context of the technologies and markets and the alternative labor supplies in the industries in which many immigrants are employed.

The argument is developed initially through a detailed study of the restaurant industry in New York City. This industry was chosen for several reasons. In cities with significant foreign-born populations, immigrants are disproportionately employed in restaurants. But the industry also employs members of many other groups, particularly teenagers and native-born women. A study of restaurants, therefore, offers an opportunity to observe the interactions of all of these groups in one industry. The restaurant industry is also characterized by a diversity of production processes and types of ownership (sole proprietors, partnerships, corporations, franchises, and large chains). Moreover, training is carried out through an assortment of processes. In the past, skill acquisition was primarily informal and unorganized, but over the past twenty years, a tier of employment has developed that requires formal training in cooking and management. As will be seen, this diversity in training, production processes, and ownership is the key to revealing the contrasting roles of immigrant and native workers.

Although the book initially focuses on the restaurant industry, examples from the construction, retail food, and garment-manufacturing industries are also presented. The argument is developed, for the purposes of generalization, in order to disclose the underlying technological, market, and social factors on which the conclusions depend. The labor market in New York City, due to its large and varied foreign-born population, is an excellent site for a study of immigrant employment. Furthermore, many of the trends in New York City's economy over the past fifteen years have foreshadowed similar trends, albeit less pronounced, in other major metropolitan centers as well as in the U.S. economy as a whole.

In addition to immigrants, the book also focuses on three other demographically defined groups: native-born teenagers, adult women, and adult black men. Although in this book each of these groups is sometimes treated as a whole, the diversity within each must be kept in mind. Differences in education constitute one particularly important factor, and as is the case with immigrants, the book's argument refers primarily to adult women and black men with low levels of educational attainment. Thus immigration clearly has a different impact on the employment of black college graduates and women with professional degrees than on high school dropouts from either group.

Finally, throughout most of the book, no distinction is made between undocumented workers, resident aliens, and naturalized citizens. This aggregation is justified in Chapter 8, in which I argue that legal status itself is not a fundamental determinant of the labor market role and impact of immigrants. Characteristics that determine the particular role of the foreign born are shared by legal and illegal immigrants and the argument developed here applies to both groups.

The Restaurant Industry

This section presents an overview of the restaurant industry. Its purpose is to provide the necessary background and context for the more focused references to the industry that occur throughout the book.

The spectacular growth of a few national fast-food chains over the past twenty years has brought the restaurant industry to the attention of the U.S. public not only as consumers but also as employees. Because of the continued growth of these chains throughout every recession since 1970, fast-food employment has, for many, come to symbolize the type of work that in an emerging postindustrial economy will be available to the unskilled and those without postsecondary education. Indeed, it may be that at any given time, more individuals work for the McDonald's Corporation or its franchise-holders than any other single corporation in the United States, and a stint behind a fast-food counter has almost become a rite of passage for teenagers from all social strata.

Employment data support the impression of rapid growth that emerges from the fast-food industry's advertising blitz. Between 1970 and 1985, restaurant employment grew three-and-one-half times as fast as total employment in the United States—131.1 percent and 38.3 percent respectively.[24] During that period, the industry accounted for over 12 percent of all employment growth in the country.[25] By 1985, restaurants provided 22 percent more jobs than the construction industry. Food-service employers reported two-and-one-half times as many employees as all primary metal and fabricated metal industries combined, and total employment in all industries manufacturing transportation vehicles was only 35 percent of total restaurant employment.

The expansion of the industry's employment during the 1970s coincided with the rapid growth of female labor force participation, the bulge in the cohorts of teenagers and young adults in their early twenties, and in some areas, the resurgence of immigration. In New York City, for example, by 1970, when the foreign born accounted for 18 percent of the city's population,[26] they comprised 40 percent of the restaurant labor force, and 10 percent of all male immigrant labor force participants were employed in restaurants. By 1980, when the city's foreign-born population had risen to 25 percent of the total, immigrants accounted for 54 percent of all restaurant workers in New York City.[27]

Indeed, the restaurant industry has become an increasing source of employment for all groups of workers who provide labor for low-wage jobs. By 1980, it accounted for 18 percent of all teenage employment in the country while the entire retail sector, which shares many of the

TABLE 1.1
Restaurant Industry (SIC 58) Demographics, by Sex and Age, 1980
(in percentages)

Sex and Age	United States		New York SMSA	
	Restaurants	All Industries	Restaurants	All Industries
Male	40.4	57.4	66.3	55.1
16–19	13.8	3.7	7.7	2.1
20–24	7.8	7.5	9.3	5.7
Female	59.6	42.6	33.7	44.9
16–19	17.0	3.4	6.1	2.2
20–24	12.2	6.7	6.2	5.9
Black	8.1	9.6	10.3	14.9
Male	3.5	4.8	6.1	8.7
Female	4.6	4.8	4.2	6.2

Source: United States data from U.S. Bureau of the Census, *Census of Population: 1980, Detailed Population Characteristics, U.S. Summary Section A: United States*, PC 80-1-D1-A (Washington, D.C.: GPO), tables 287 and 289. New York SMSA data from U.S. Bureau of the Census, *Census of Population: 1980, Detailed Population Characteristics, New York*, PC 80-1-D34 (Washington, D.C.: GPO) tables 228 and 230.

employment and labor characteristics of the restaurant industry, accounted for close to one-half of all teenage employment.[28]

In 1980, 2.5 million women worked in the industry and restaurants accounted for 6 percent of all female employment, 4 percent of all employment for black women, and 3 percent for black men.[29] Table 1.1 presents a demographic summary of the industry's labor force in the United States and in New York in 1980.

Twenty years ago the industry relied primarily on informal, on-the-job training to produce its skilled workers and even its entrepreneurial cadre. This has changed. Although many low-skilled jobs remain, the industry increasingly has turned to formally trained personnel to cook food and particularly to manage restaurants. At the same time, cooking technology has moved more of the production process out of the restaurants themselves and into manufacturing-type operations where raw food is at least partially processed. This trend, along with other factors such as suburbanization and the automobile, has resulted in an employment structure in the food-service industry characterized, on the one hand, by large numbers of unskilled, part-time, high-turnover, lower-level workers and, on the other hand, by formally trained managers and other higher-level workers who use modern food production, managerial, and organizational procedures.

The case study on which the analysis is based used data from the U.S. Census, the Bureau of Labor Statistics, other government agencies, and available secondary sources. In addition, structured but open-ended interviews were conducted in 1981 with ninety restaurant owners and managers in New York City. The selection of the sample is explained in Appendix A. In addition, telephone interviews were conducted with a 2 percent random sample of restaurants listed in the New York Telephone Company yellow pages and located in three New York City boroughs—Manhattan, Brooklyn, and Queens. The owners or managers of these restaurants were asked a short list of questions about the nativity of the owner or owners, the type of cuisine and service, and the establishment's general price range.

Based on the information gathered from these surveys, a classification system for the industry was developed. Restaurants were categorized into one of four distinct sectors that differ in production processes and personnel procedures, the roles immigrants play in each sector, and the demographic groups forming the core of its labor force. The four sectors are referred to as the fast-food, full-service, intermediate, and immigrant sectors. (Table 1.2 displays the basic characteristics of the sectors.)

The fast-food sector represents the forefront of the recent trends in restaurant technology and employment. It is dominated by large corporations and employs large numbers of unskilled workers supervised by managers who receive formal training. Nationally its market share is over 40 percent. Whereas the sector uses production processes based on low-skilled employees, it uses relatively few immigrants, primarily employing native teenagers, even in cities with large immigrant populations.

The full-service sector is characterized by full table service, menus, and food preparation processes that require developed and versatile kitchen skills. The restaurants in this sector have extensive menus, make little use of prepared foods, and are still predominantly independently owned. Nationally the sector accounts for about 10 percent of the restaurant market.

In most full-service restaurants, technology and production methods have changed little over the past twenty years. Some labor-saving machines have been developed and there have been advances in stove and oven technology, but these innovations have not resulted in the qualitative changes in production wrought by technological development in the fast-food sector. Full-service restaurants still start with unprocessed raw food, which is washed and prepared initially by unskilled or semiskilled workers, cooked by workers of various skill levels depending on the restaurant, and served by waiters and

TABLE 1.2
Restaurant Industry Sectors

Sector	Turnover	Workweek	Characteristics Labor Force U.S.	New York	Market Share U.S.	New York	Price Range	Labor Share of Sales
Fast-food	High	Part-time	Teenagers	Teenagers	.40	.25	Low	.15–.20
Intermediate	Moderate	Part-time	Women	Women and immigrants	.40–.45	.15	Low to Moderate	.20–.30
Full-service	Low	Full-time	Adult men and women	Adult men and immigrants	.10	.20	Moderate to High	.40–.50
Immigrant	Low	Full-time	Immigrants	Immigrants	.05–.10	.40	Low to High	N.A.

Source: Thomas R. Bailey, "Labor Market Competition and Economic Mobility in Low Wage Employment: A Case Study of Immigrants in the Restaurant Industry" (Ph.D. dissertation, Economics Department, Massachusetts Institute of Technology, 1983), chapter 5. For labor shares, see D. Daryl Wyckoff and W. Earl Sasser, *The Chain Restaurant Industry* (Lexington, Mass.: Lexington Books, 1978), p. xlviii.

waitresses. The labor share in total sales, which has been estimated at 38.5 percent (over 45 percent if tips are included) is therefore higher in this sector than in other sectors. Immigrants play an important role in the industry in New York City, particularly as skilled and unskilled kitchen workers.

Thus, full-service restaurants have been more resistant than the industry as a whole to the central trends in restaurant management, personnel, and production. Full-service establishments continue to rely on full-time adult workers, and cooking skills are still important. Nevertheless, restaurants in this sector have not escaped the influence of the recent trends in the industry. Formal training of both cooks and managers is increasingly important, and production technologies and organizational and business practices allow some simplification of cooking techniques.

The labor process in the intermediate sector lies between the processes that predominate in the full-service and fast-food sectors. Although there is a trend towards standardization and skill reduction and although chains are becoming more important, the intermediate sector is less resistant to the revolving-door employment that characterizes the fast-food sector. The intermediate sector employs immigrants as cooks and dishwashers, but nationally the sector relies primarily on adult women. It accounts for about 40 percent of the restaurant market in the country.

Restaurants in the immigrant sector are defined by foreign-born ownership. Although they serve all levels of the market, their production processes and technologies are most similar to those used in the full-service sector. Almost all workers in immigrant restaurants are themselves immigrants. This sector accounts for close to one-half of the market in New York City.

The following classification criteria were used: All restaurants owned by foreign-born individuals were classified as immigrant restaurants; restaurants without waiter or waitress service as fast-food outlets; establishments with table service and with an average check of $8 or less in 1981 as intermediate restaurants; and more expensive restaurants were categorized as full-service establishments.

Outline of the Book

My basic strategy in this book is to compare the employment roles of immigrants and native teenagers, adult women and adult black men, and develop the implications of these differences for competition between the groups. Chapters 2 and 3 lay the groundwork for the argument by examining the characteristics of immigrant employment.

In Chapter 2, I discuss immigrant employment in the restaurant industry, particularly in the full-service sector, which illustrates one type of role that immigrant workers commonly fill and explains why they play that particular role. In Chapter 3, the immigrant sector of the restaurant industry is discussed to illustrate the role of the foreign born both as workers and as entrepreneurs in immigrant-owned businesses. The chapter ends with a discussion of immigrant employment and ownership in the garment industry as an additional illustration of the argument. In Chapter 4, I contrast the roles of immigrants in the restaurant industry to those of native teenagers and women. The fast-food sector is used as an example of employment dominated by teenagers while the analysis of the intermediate sector is used to elucidate the role of adult women. The chapter includes another example of the employment of teenagers, drawn from the retail food industry. The causes of the contrasting roles and their implications for competition between immigrants and these native groups are addressed in Chapter 5. I take a similar approach to the interactions between native black men and immigrants by examining, in Chapter 6, the contrasts between them in the restaurant and construction industries and by analyzing, in Chapter 7, the causes of the differences and the nature of the competition between the two groups. The argument of Chapter 8 is that the book's thesis applies to undocumented immigrants as well as to legal resident aliens and naturalized citizens. Finally, in Chapter 9, I summarize the substantive conclusions and suggest some implications for immigration policy.

Notes

1. Throughout this book, the terms "immigrant" and "foreign born" are used interchangeably. These terms refer to undocumented workers as well as to legal resident aliens and naturalized citizens.

2. Vernon M. Briggs, *Immigration Policy and the American Labor Force* (Baltimore, Md.: Johns Hopkins University Press, 1984), p. 163.

3. Briggs, 1984, Chapter 8.

4. Michael Piore, *Birds of Passage: Migrant Labor and Industrial Societies* (New York, N.Y.: Cambridge University Press, 1979), chapter 3.

5. George E. Johnson, "The Labor Market Effects of Immigration," *Industrial and Labor Relations Review* 33 (April 1980): 331–341; Barry R. Chiswick, "The Impact of Immigration on the Level and Distribution of Economic Well-Being," in Barry R. Chiswick, ed., *The Gateway* (Washington D.C.: American Enterprise Institute, 1982), pp. 289–314; and Michael Wachter, "The Labor Market and Illegal Immigration: The Outlook for the 1980s," *Industrial and Labor Relations Review* 33 (April 1980): 343–354.

6. The extent of these gains and losses depends on the assumptions about the elasticities of supply and substitution between the various factors of production and other influences such as the minimum wage. For example, George Johnson assumes that unskilled workers and skilled workers are complementary and that the labor supply for unskilled workers is inelastic. He therefore concludes that immigration will have little displacement effect and that native skilled workers benefit from immigration. For a discussion of the sensitivity of conclusions about the impact of immigration to changes in the assumptions about elasticities, see John K. Hill, "The Economic Impact of Tighter U.S. Border Security," *Economic Review: The Federal Reserve Bank of Dallas* (July 1985): 12–20. Bailey also analyzes the sensitivity of these conclusions to changes in the elasticities, although immigrants are not assumed to be perfect substitutes for low-skilled natives. See Thomas R. Bailey, "Labor Market Competition and Economic Mobility in Low Wage Employment: A Case Study of Immigrants in the Restaurant Industry" (PhD dissertation, Economics Department, Massachusetts Institute of Technology, 1983).

7. Barry R. Chiswick, "Is the New Immigration Less Skilled than the Old?" *Journal of Labor Economics* 4 (April 1986): 168–192.

8. Gregory DeFreitas, "The Impact of Immigration on Low-Wage Workers" (Department of Economics, Barnard College, March 1985), unpublished; and Chiswick, 1986.

9. According to the 1980 census, 28.6 percent of employed natives in New York City were in professional/managerial positions, 27.9 percent in administrative support, 12.1 percent in service, and 5.3 in operative positions. But only 19.9 percent of the foreign born were in professional/managerial positions, 17.4 percent in administrative support, 18.4 percent in service, and 14.1 percent in operative positions. The differences between foreign born and native born in these occupations are even greater if the comparison is restricted to the immigrants who arrived between 1965 and 1980. U.S. Bureau of the Census, *Census of Population: 1980, Public Use Microdata Samples (A Sample), New York* (Washington, D.C.: GPO).

10. U.S. Department of Labor, Bureau of Labor Statistics, *Geographic Profile of Employment and Unemployment, 1984,* bulletin no. 2234 (Washington, D.C.: GPO, 1985), tables 1 and 2.

11. One study by Barton Smith and Robert Newman based on the 1970 census found that after controlling for sex, race, age, marital status, education, and occupation, the earnings of workers living in cities in Texas near the Mexican border were 8 percent lower than the earnings of Texans living in Houston, which is farther from the border. The Houston residents also earned more when the sample was divided into subgroups of Mexican Americans, age groups, high- and low-wage earners, and high- and low-skilled workers. The negative impact was strongest for Mexican Americans and low-skilled workers. In this study, the distance from the border was assumed to measure the strength of the impact of immigrants on the labor market. Another study by Jean Grossman found moderate substitutability between the foreign born and second and higher generation natives. And Gregory DeFreitas and Adriana

Marshall found a small negative relationship between the growth rate of manufacturing wages in SMSAs between 1970 and 1980 and the proportion of all manufacturing jobs held by the foreign born in 1980, although data limitations prevented the authors from examining the effects on native manufacturing wages alone. Barton Smith and Robert Newman, "Depressed Wages along the U.S.-Mexico Border: An Empirical Analysis," *Economic Inquiry* 15 (January 1977): 51–66; Jean Grossman, "The Substitutability of Natives and Immigrants in Production," *Review of Economics and Statistics* 64 (October 1982): 596–603; Gregory DeFreitas and Adriana Marshall, "Immigration and Wage Growth in U.S. Manufacturing in the 1970s," Industrial Relations Research Association Series, Proceedings of the Thirty-Sixth Annual Meeting, 1983, pp. 148–156.

12. For example, Allan King concluded that the presence of foreign-born Hispanic males had no negative effect on the wages of second and higher generation Hispanic males. Thomas Muller and Thomas Espenshade found no relationship between the presence of Hispanics and the unemployment of black males. And George Borjas has reported on two studies of the problem, one on the relationships among Hispanics, black, and white (all other) males and the other on the relationships among Hispanic and non-Hispanic immigrants, native black and Hispanic men and native women. He found that there was competition only between immigrants and native women and that immigrants strengthen the employment position of native black men. Allan King, "The Effect of Undocumented Hispanic Workers on the Earnings of Hispanic Americans," paper prepared for the Workshop on Labor Market Impacts of Immigrants, Wingspread Conference Center, Racine, Wisc., August 3–6, 1982, sponsored by the Rockefeller Foundation. Thomas Muller and Thomas Espenshade, *The Fourth Wave: California's Newest Immigrants* (Washington, D.C.: The Urban Institute, 1985), p. 101; George Borjas, "The Substitutability of Blacks, Hispanics and White Labor," *Economic Inquiry* 21 (1983): 93–106; and George Borjas, "The Demographic Determinants of the Demand for Black Labor," in Richard B. Freeman and Harry J. Holzer, ed., *The Black Youth Employment Crisis* (Chicago, Ill.: University of Chicago Press, 1986), pp. 191–230.

13. Many of the studies use imprecise proxies, such as the distance from the border, to measure the presence of immigrants (Smith and Newman, 1977) or the Hispanic population (Borjas, 1983; Muller and Espenshade, 1985). DeFreitas and Marshall (1983) do not differentiate between the changes in native wages and those in average wage levels. For a discussion of methodological issues involved in the production function techniques used by Grossman (1982) and Borjas (1983, 1986), see James H. Grant and Daniel S. Hamermesh, "Labor Market Competition among Youths, White Women and Others," *Review of Economics and Statistics* 63 (August 1981): 354–360. For a general review of the empirical research in this area see Michael Greenwood and John M. McDowell, "The Factor Market Consequences of U.S. Immigration," *Journal of Economic Literature* 24 (December 1986): 1738–1772.

14. It is interesting that although the skill level is the theoretical basis of the analysis, most empirical work in this field ignores the issue of skill. These

studies simply divide people into demographic groups and measure their impact on each other. No attempt is made to justify why these groups should play different roles in the labor market. Therefore, research on labor market competition is either empirical analysis of the interactions of immigrants and other demographic groups with no grounding in theory—because the theory does not recognize the distinction between the groups and indeed points to skill differences that are ignored in the research—or theoretical analysis in which the prediction that there will be displacement is built into the model—because aggregating immigrants and other groups as unskilled workers is equivalent to assuming that these groups are perfect substitutes.

15. Piore, 1979, p. 54.

16. According to Piore, the separation of the sectors is based on technological and market characteristics and therefore is not affected by changes in the relative supplies of various types of workers. He argues that productivity is related to the extent of the market, the standardization of output, and the stability of demand. Furthermore, demand can be divided into stable and unstable components. Firms using the most advanced technologies are more efficient than their competition, but in order to achieve this efficiency they must invest in specialized and inflexible equipment. If demand falls off, these machines cannot be shifted to other functions. Thus the most efficient firms serve the stable component of demand, whereas the unstable component is served by firms that use a more flexible technology and that rely more on labor. Technologically advanced firms are large, have stable markets, long-term planning horizons, and high productivity. They can therefore afford to provide stable employment, higher wages, and opportunities for advancement. For peripheral firms, unstable employment and low wages are preconditions for survival. See Suzanne Berger and Michael Piore, *Dualism and Discontinuity in Industrial Societies* (New York, N.Y.: Cambridge University Press, 1980), chapter 3.

17. From this perspective, the segmented labor market model predicts more job displacement of low-skilled or secondary-sector workers than is implied by the conventional economic model. Conventional economists argue that supply and demand determine wage and employment levels. Segmentation theorists argue that aggregate demand determines employment levels and that institutional factors, such as the minimum wage, determine wage levels. See Eileen Applebaum, "The Labor Market in Post Keynesian Theory," in Michael Piore, ed., *Unemployment and Inflation: Institutionalist and Structuralist Views* (White Plains, N.Y.: M. E. Sharpe, Inc., 1979). Thus in the segmented labor market model, when a shortage of labor exists for a given output and wage level, immigration is initiated to fill the gap, but when a surplus of labor exists there is no mechanism to increase the number of jobs, and each additional worker simply adds to unemployment. At least the wage responses assumed in neoclassical theory would result in employment expansion due to lower wages.

18. Stanley Leiberson, *A Piece of the Pie: Black and White Immigrants Since 1880* (Berkeley, Cal.: University of California Press, 1980); and Thomas Sowell, *Ethnic America: A History* (New York, N.Y.: Basic Books, 1981).

19. Geoffrey Carliner, "Wages, Earnings, and Hours of First, Second and Third Generation American Males," *Economic Inquiry* 18 (January 1980): 87–102; Barry R. Chiswick, "The Effect of Americanization on the Earnings of Foreign-Born Men," *Journal of Political Economy* 86 (October 1978): 897–921; Gregory DeFreitas, "The Earnings of Immigrants in the American Labor Market" (PhD dissertation, Department of Economics, Columbia University, 1979); James E. Long, "The Effect of Americanization on Earnings: Some Evidence for Women," *Journal of Political Economy* 88 (June 1980): 620–629; and C. Matthew Snipp and Marta Tienda, "Chicano Occupational Mobility," *Social Science Quarterly* 65 (June 1984): 364–380.

20. Although this conclusion about immigrant adaptation has been challenged recently by Borjas, its congruence with the optimistic view of earlier immigration will make it difficult to dislodge as the conventional wisdom. George Borjas, "Assimilation, Changes in Cohort Quality, and Earnings of Immigrants," *Journal of Labor Economics* 3 (October 1985): 463–489. See Greenwood and McDowell, 1986, for a review of this controversy.

21. A very partial list of this research includes: Howard Aldrich and Albert Reiss, Jr., "Continuities in the Study of Ecological Succession: Changes in Race Composition of Neighborhoods and their Businesses," *American Journal of Sociology* 81 (1976): 846–866; Edna Bonacich, Ivan Light, and Charles C. Wong, "Korean Immigrant Small Business in Los Angeles," in R. Bryce-Laporte, ed., *A Sourcebook on the New Immigration* (New Brunswick, N.J.: Transaction, 1980); Edna Bonacich and John Modell, *The Economic Basis of Ethnic Solidarity* (Berkeley, Cal.: University of California Press, 1980); and Ivan H. Light, *Ethnic Enterprise in America: Business and Welfare Among Chinese, Japanese, and Blacks* (Berkeley, Cal.: University of California Press, 1972). For a critical review of the literature on entrepreneurship, see Roger Waldinger, *Through the Eye of the Needle: Immigrant Enterprise in New York's Garment Trades* (New York, N.Y.: New York University Press, 1986). Frank Fratoe has compiled a collection of abstracts of dozens of articles and books on minority entrepreneurship and has produced a synthesis and overview of that research. See Frank A. Fratoe, *Abstracts of the Sociological Literature on Minority Business Ownership* (Washington, D.C.: Research Division, Office of Advocacy, Research and Information, Minority Business Development Agency, U.S. Department of Commerce, November 1984), and *Sociological Perspectives on Minority Business Ownership: A Synthesis of the Literature with Research and Policy Implications* (Washington, D.C.: Research Division, Office of Advocacy, Research and Information, Minority Business Development Agency, U.S. Department of Commerce, December 1984).

22. Kenneth L. Wilson and Alejandro Portes, "Immigrant Enclaves: An Analysis of the Labor Market Experiences of Cubans in Miami," *American Journal of Sociology* 86 (September 1980): 295–319.

23. Suzanne Model, "A Comparative Perspective on the Ethnic Enclave: Blacks, Italians, and Jews in New York City," *International Migration Review* 19 (Spring 1985): 65–81; Alejandro Portes and Robert L. Bach, *Latin Journey: Cuban and Mexican Immigrants in the United States* (Berkeley, Cal.: University of California Press, 1985); Waldinger, 1986; and Kenneth L. Wilson

and W. Allan Martin, "Ethnic Enclaves: A Comparison of the Cuban and Black Economies in Miami," *American Journal of Sociology* 88 (1982): 135–160.

24. Data in this and the following paragraph are from U.S. Department of Labor, Bureau of Labor Statistics, *Employment and Earnings*, March 1971, table B-2, and March 1986, table B-2.

25. If data are adjusted for average weekly hours, relative growth of the industry is somewhat lower. Thus restaurants accounted for 10 percent of all growth in hours of employment.

26. U.S. Bureau of the Census, *Census of Population: 1970, Subject Reports, Final Report, PC(2)-1A, National Origin and Language* (Washington, D.C.: GPO), table 81.

27. U.S. Bureau of the Census, *Census of Population: 1970, Public Use Samples of Basic Records (5 percent Sample), New York* (Washington, D.C.: GPO); and U.S. Bureau of the Census, *Census of Population: 1980.*

28. U.S. Bureau of the Census, *Census of Population: 1980, Detailed Population Characteristics, United States Summary Section A: United States, PC80-1-D1-A* (Washington, D.C.: GPO), table 289.

29. U.S. Bureau of the Census, *Census of Population: 1980,* table 287.

2

Immigrant Workers and the Immigration Process

Dishwashers, janitors and cleaners, low-skilled machine operators and factory hands, newsstand clerks—these are the types of jobs in which recent immigrants appear to be concentrated in many of the largest industrial sectors in the United States. Indeed, U.S. census data show immigrant overrepresentation among service workers and operatives and in nondurable manufacturing, retail trade, and personal services.[1]

Although there is no gainsaying the large numbers of unskilled and low-skilled jobs held by the foreign born, skill level is only one dimension of employment. The conception of the labor process as simply the employment of individuals of various skill levels is a narrow one indeed. For each individual, work is one among a set of competing activities. The mobilization of labor involves more than a technological relationship among skills, machines, and materials; it is fundamentally shaped by the interactions between workers and the broad social and institutional context within which work occurs. Moreover, the labor process not only involves the use of skills in the production of goods and services but is also itself a crucial process in the reproduction of required skills.

If these factors shape the labor process and the roles of workers and groups of workers, then they also influence the interaction between workers and the extent to which workers compete. In this chapter, I look beyond skill levels to identify the particular roles that immigrants play in the labor market. I analyze the employment of immigrants in the restaurant industry, focusing on the industry's full-service sector. In the second part of the chapter, I identify the causes that lead immigrants to hold their particular positions in this industry. In subsequent chapters, I shall compare immigrant and native workers.

The Restaurant Industry

The production and labor process in the restaurant industry is experiencing two central trends. On the one hand, the industry has increased its reliance on short-term, part-time workers with minimal skills. This trend has accompanied the spread of fast-food technology at the low end of the market and the introduction of standardization and simplification of cooking and food-preparation techniques in the middle levels of the market and to some extent, even at the upper end. On the other hand, managerial positions at all levels of the industry and cooking positions in the middle- and upper-market strata have increasingly required formal postsecondary education and often specialized managerial or restaurant training.

The role of immigrant workers in the restaurant industry runs against these central trends. The foreign born, with the exception of Europeans, are found primarily in two areas. The first area includes those sectors and occupations that do not operate easily within the labor process defined by the industry's central technological and organizational thrust. These occupations include the unskilled and semiskilled positions in the full-service sector and the upper end of the intermediate sector and most of the positions in the relatively expensive immigrant-owned establishments. The functions carried out by workers in these positions are not susceptible to automation of the fast-food variety. Restaurateurs have not turned to formally trained workers either because in the case of low-skilled workers, formal training is unnecessary or because in the case of cooks in ethnic restaurants, formally trained workers are not available. Thus, most of the dishwashers and porters in New York City's full-service sector are immigrants, with a large proportion from the Dominican Republic. Other Latin American countries, the West Indies, several Asian countries, and the Middle East are all well represented in this cadre of workers.

The second area in which immigrants are concentrated is the sectors and occupations that could use emerging production processes but employ immigrants in order to resist the industry's central technological, organizational, and personnel trends. This occurs most commonly in restaurants owned by immigrants. Thus, although the new technologies and labor processes have had their greatest impact at the low end of the market, cheap immigrant restaurants, employing immigrant workers exclusively, have been able to compete successfully by using more traditional production processes. And although formal training for skilled positions in the full-service sector has grown rapidly, many immigrants who learned their skills informally also fill these jobs. The first area of immigrant concentration—the full-service restaurants—is the subject of this chapter, and the second area—immigrant-owned restaurants—will be discussed in Chapter 3.

Full-Service Restaurants

Despite the common image of low-level, low-skilled restaurant employment, the full-service sector exhibits a production process and job structure that are more complicated than those of other sectors. In full-service kitchens, there is an articulated skill hierarchy that includes unskilled workers and, in some restaurants, skilled workers with formal training and extensive experience. There is also a range of skills in the dining room, although compared to the kitchen, fewer skills are necessary at the upper end of the dining room hierarchy. In the following sections, particular aspects of the full-service employment process are discussed. These factors distinguish the sector from the fast-food and intermediate sectors and highlight the differences between the roles of immigrant and of native workers.

Turnover and Hours

Full-service restaurants require skilled workers with adequate experience. In contrast to some cooking jobs in the other sectors, short-term part-timers cannot be counted on to fill positions in full-service establishments. Even the unskilled work force in the full-service sector is characterized by low turnover. New York City managers interviewed for this study reported that many of their low-level workers had long tenure. For example, one owner said that not one of his eleven kitchen workers had left in the preceding three years. Another owner said that his day-shift turnover was only 5 percent. According to him, "You couldn't beat them out with a stick." Still another owner reported that most of his dishwashers had been there for several years. Only three out of nineteen full-service managers complained that turnover in the kitchen was high, although even high average turnover rates can obscure underlying stability. Many of the workers who are fired or quit are short-tenure workers who do not work out. A typical pattern is that several workers are hired in sequence for a particular position until one stays permanently.

Although it is easy to find unskilled workers to fill openings, managers of full-service restaurants avoid the revolving-door employment process that is characteristic of the fast-food sector.

Hiring and screening workers is time-consuming and risky. Fast-food chains can derive economies of scale through centralized hiring that is not available to small independent restaurants. Furthermore, full-service restaurants succeed or fail on the quality of their food and service; managers need to concentrate on these aspects of the business in order to satisfy customers and maintain the restaurant's reputation. They do not want to expend much effort in searching for dishwashers and porters.

Full-service restaurants also have a more rigid job structure than fast-food outlets. Because workers are not interchangeable, it is more disruptive when workers are missing. It is harder to find a fill-in on short notice, particularly in small restaurants, and even for unskilled positions, each restaurant has unique procedures that must be taught to newcomers. In addition, part-timers are less useful in the full-service than in the fast-food sector. Unskilled kitchen work can be distributed throughout the workday more easily than in the fast-food sector—simple food-preparation tasks can be carried out during off-hours, and dirty dishes can accumulate during peak periods.

Paternalism

The management of unskilled workers in the full-service sector is often paternalistic. Consistent with its evocation of the father's traditional role in the family, paternalism is often understood to be a system in which the owner has final and arbitrary authority but exercises it for the benefit of the employees. The term as it is used here refers to a system in which, although the owners or managers are unencumbered by formal rules regarding pay, fringe benefits, or work organization and do maintain ultimate authority, their actions are nonetheless constrained to some extent by an implicit understanding concerning the rights and obligations of employees. One important characteristic of paternalistic systems is the personal relationship between owner and employee. Furthermore, as Tony Lawson notes, "essentially paternal employers attempt to join family and work symbolically with themselves as the authority."[2]

The concept of paternalistic or "traditional" authority structures dates from Max Weber. According to Weber:

> Obedience [under traditional authority] is not owed to enacted rules, but to the person who occupies a position of authority by tradition or who has been chosen for such a position on a traditional basis. His commands are legitimized in one of two ways: (a) partly in terms of traditions which themselves directly determine the content of the command and the objects and extent of authority. In so far as this is true, to overstep the

traditional limitations would endanger his traditional status by undermining acceptance of his legitimacy. (b) In part, it is a matter of the chief's free personal decision, in that tradition leaves a certain sphere open for this. [3]

To a greater or lesser extent all discussions of paternalism as a management style have recognized these two aspects of paternalistic systems. Over time though, the understanding of the social basis of paternalism has changed.

For Weber, who associated capitalism with technical-bureaucratic authority and organization, the bases were traditional precapitalistic relationships. Reinhard Bendix focused the analysis of traditional authority more directly on the workplace. The basis of the nineteenth-century paternalist firm was the traditional notion that the rich needed to take care of the poor. [4] Nevertheless, Bendix did argue that traditionalism "frequently facilitated the management of labor." He went on to say that "the workers' widespread reluctance to change a customary way of life could also benefit an employer if the relations between them were stabilized by family ties and reciprocal loyalties." [5] Nevertheless, both because paternalism stood in the way of full capitalist development and because there were strong forces pushing it toward outright exploitation, he suggested that it would decline in importance. [6]

More recently scholars have argued that the small firm not characterized by formal bureaucratic authority has an enduring place in the modern economy. [7] Thus Richard Edwards drew on Weber's concept of traditional authority to characterize the mode of control in secondary-sector jobs. [8] Such jobs, he argued, accounted for as much as one-third of all jobs in the U.S. economy. [9] But if traditional authority is to remain an important factor in the labor process in a modern economy, its social basis can no longer lie, as Weber and Bendix argued, in the traditional precapitalist hierarchical class structure. In this light it is not surprising that Edwards referred to Weber's concept of charismatic authority, which relied less on historically specific circumstances than on the concept of traditional authority. But in fact, Edwards's work, as well as earlier studies of segmented labor markets, emphasized the arbitrary and authoritarian character of traditional authority and downplayed the notion that those in authority were constrained by mutual obligations to their subordinates. Rather, authority in the secondary sector was based on the greater power that resulted from capitalist control of the means of production. Thus paternalism, or at least paternalism based on the Weberian concept of traditional authority, slipped from segmentation models. In these models, the secondary sector was characterized by nonbureaucratic control, or simple control as Edwards put it, bereft of traditional constraints. The high turnover that supposedly characterized the secondary sector prevented the development of long-term stable relationships and thereby thwarted the establishment of customary obligations. In fact, it was in the primary sector, where workers tended to be attached to one job for long periods, in which custom was believed to play an important role.[10]

But in the past few years, this view has been questioned even by those working within the segmentation framework. First, some studies have found that although turnover in the secondary sector is higher than in the primary sector, the difference is not so large as the early formulations had suggested.[11] Edwards hypothesized that turnover in the secondary sector is held down because workers fear not being able to find another job. But case studies have also revealed that despite low wages and restricted mobility opportunities, many workers in low-quality jobs do not exhibit alienation or resentment and they often express loyalty to the firm and high levels of identification with the interests of the firm.[12] The authors of these studies argue that these conditions reflect the use of paternalism as a technique for controlling and motivating workers.

What emerges from the studies, as well as from interviews with full-service and immigrant restaurant owners conducted for this project, is a picture of a system in which workers, in exchange for certain obligations of the employer, are expected to be loyal, dependable, and willing to work overtime and extra shifts. The central obligation of the paternalistic owner appears to be the provision of job security. In fact, as Lawson pointed out, the system is most seriously threatened when business conditions or technological change require long-term and significant labor force cuts and layoffs.[13] Thus employers who try to establish a paternalistic system often adjust hours, share work, and reorganize their production before they actually cut their staffs. Peter Doeringer reported on employers in Maine who laid off workers in such a way as to ensure that they would be eligible for unemployment compensation.[14] Similarly, full-service managers often reported the use of work sharing. As one said, "During slack periods, we do more cleaning."

In addition to job security, another obligation of paternalistic owners involves management style and supervision. Owners know the workers, address them by their first names, help them with financial problems, and sometimes let them take off time for personal affairs, such as out-of-town performances for actors and trips home for immigrants. They at least claim that they treat their employees with respect.

Thus paternalism in the workplace as it is defined here is similar to Weber's original formulation of traditional authority in that it combines the arbitrary authority of the owner with implied mutual obligations. Following Bendix, it is an efficient personnel system under some conditions, although contrary to his implication, those conditions are not disappearing. And modern paternalism is not based on a traditional hierarchical class structure in which the upper classes are obliged to care for the lower; rather it is based on an implicit agreement between employer and worker in which the worker trades dependability and flexibility for job security and a less alienating and unpleasant social environment at work,[15] although conflicts of interest certainly remain.

Like any approach to management, the attractiveness of a paternalistic system depends on its relative costs and benefits. In this case, in spite of higher wage bills during slack periods, a loss of flexibility, and the cost of some discretionary benefits or favors, the owner benefits from lower costs associated with turnover and from increases in productivity. With respect to workers in jobs with restricted opportunities for occupational mobility, this system of motivation works only for those workers who have limited aspirations.

Network Hiring

Thus far, I have discussed paternalistic personnel policy based on a traditional hierarchical class structure and on what amounts to an implicit agreement between employer and worker. In the latter case, the relationships on which the system depends originate within the workplace after the worker is hired. But family, ethnic, or personal ties that exist outside of the workplace are a third basis for paternalism. In general, such outside relationships do not exist in the full-service sector in which owners and low-level workers almost always have different ethnic, social, and even linguistic characteristics. Nevertheless, full-service restaurant managers usually do try to import outside social relationships through the use of network hiring—recruiting the friends and relatives of current employees. Almost all of the full-service sector managers who were interviewed for this study relied primarily on this form of hiring. Some restaurants even use an extreme version that resembles subcontracting. For example, in one restaurant, a Chinese dishwasher acted as a crew chief and filled openings for dishwashers and busboys from among his friends and family.

Network hiring has several advantages for the employer. When it is used, the new recruits are never completely unknown. Network hiring also eases training because the intermediary who acts as recruiter often takes responsibility for showing the new employee the particular routines of the restaurant. The relationships that originate outside the workplace constrain the behavior of the new worker both because the old worker has some implicit responsibility to oversee the work of the recruit and because the latter realizes that his work reflects on the recruiter. Hence, it is likely that at least initially, the new worker will be more dependable. For these reasons, network hiring mitigates turnover costs and is a partial alternative to wage increases as a strategy for establishing stability and continuity in the workplace.[16] It is also a cheap and effective method of finding replacements; when the labor market is tight, it can be used to locate workers who may be out of the local labor force—workers from the home countries of current immigrant employees. Finally, helping out the family and friends of their employees reinforces the paternalistic atmosphere that many owners try to develop.

For the employer, nevertheless, there are disadvantages to network hiring. Although networks may help ensure dependability among employees, they also promote solidaristic behavior, which tends to constrain the employer. Concepts of fairness and equity become more influential as the social relationships within the workplace strengthen. For example, one employer who owned several restaurants said that he usually had to pay dishwashers in his various restaurants the same wages because they often knew each other and complained if wages varied too much. Some managers said that they preferred not to have friends working together because it encouraged stealing and other forms of undesirable activity.

Although economists have long emphasized the importance of network hiring in terms of job search, recruitment, and labor market information,[17] the effects of the practice are not limited to these factors. To be sure, information is one fundamental aspect of network hiring, but outside relationships that are imported to the workplace as well as those established *in* the workplace, are also a continuing influence on the interaction between employers and workers. That is, networks are more than sources of information; they are also independent factors that constrain and shape the employment and training process.

Training

In the past, most full-service restaurants relied on informally trained cooks, although the most expensive restaurants and hotels employed European-trained chefs. But in the past fifteen years professional cooking and restaurant management schools in the United

States have multiplied. According to a survey of food-service employment opportunities by the *New York Times*, "At top professional cooking schools . . . the number of students has increased ten-fold in the last decade."[18] These schools have Ivy League level tuitions. In 1985, the New York Restaurant School charged over $5,000 for its twenty-week program and the Cornell School of Hotel Administration cost $14,000 a year for tuition, room, and board. Moreover, there are now more than 100 four-year colleges that offer degrees in restaurant and hotel management and at least 400 community colleges and vocational/technical schools with two-year programs.[19]

The development and reproduction of a skilled labor force in the restaurant industry is thwarted by low pay and disorganized, erratic training processes. In New York, the earnings of cooks vary widely, but they are low relative to earnings in other industries. According to a survey conducted in March 1983, the median straight-time weekly earnings of general cooks[20] who worked more than thirty hours a week was $207.[21] The top 25 percent earned over $290 a week. (These data are not adjusted for different workweeks except to exclude workers who worked fewer than thirty hours.) Chefs earned considerably more. Their median weekly earnings were $308. Those in the top quartile earned at least $430 a week, and the highest paid in the sample earned $1,300 a week. Short-order cooks earned an average of $4.82 an hour. (At the time of the survey, the minimum wage was $3.35 an hour.) Therefore, with the exception of about 35 percent of the chefs and a few other cooks, no workers in the industry in 1983 earned wages that if annualized would equal the 1983 average income ($21,759 a year) for workers covered by unemployment insurance in the New York metropolitan area. Data from the 1970 census support the hypothesis that training in cooking skills was a poor investment.[22] Earnings of cooks were below the earnings of workers in other occupations who had similar ages and educational attainment.

Recent developments in the industry may have improved the relative pay of cooks, especially those with formal training who are employed in better restaurants. Nevertheless, development of skills through on-the-job training continues to be hampered by the disorganized character of the skill-acquisition process itself. There are no stable and recognized structures for on-the-job skill acquisition and advancement except in a few large restaurants. Small firm size is chiefly responsible for the lack of job ladders. When a kitchen employs only a few workers, there are gaps in the skill hierarchy that cannot be bridged by experience on the job. Typically, there is an upper limit to the mobility of employees who start out as unskilled kitchen workers unless they acquire formal training or cooking experience in other restaurants. An individual restaurant, therefore, is unlikely to provide a complete job ladder. The small size of the firms and unstable profits preclude the development of special training programs that might bridge the gaps. Even when workers can learn on the job, if there are only one or two desirable positions, aspiring cooks may have long waits before their predecessors move on. For these reasons, workers must learn their skills by shifting among restaurants.[23] This, in turn, prevents the establishment of internal labor markets that strengthen the attachment of skilled workers to particular firms. Moreover, interfirm movement reduces the returns to firm-specific skills.

This need to move in order to learn also hinders the development of a paternalistic style in the management of skilled restaurant workers. Although owners might be able to offer some measure of job security, as they do for unskilled workers, they often cannot offer promotion. Because most employers cannot expect to retain their workers who want to move up, the employers have little incentive to incur the costs of training. Thus, at least for ambitious workers in this industry, the trade-off that underlies paternalistic management is less favorable than it is for those workers who have weaker aspirations.

In cases where general or transferable skills are involved, economic theory implies that workers pay training costs through lower wages, but in many restaurants, unskilled workers are already paid at a legislated or negotiated floor. There is no margin to trade lower wages for training. Furthermore, there is no guarantee that workers would be trained even if there were such a margin. Managers, with a few exceptions, evinced little interest in teaching skills other than those that are specific to their particular restaurants. In small firms, it simply is not possible to save much money by cutting the wages of one or two low-paid dishwashers. The employer is therefore unable to recoup training costs either through paying the workers less than other unskilled workers during the training process or more important, through holding onto them and paying them less than other skilled workers after training is completed. Thus, given the economics of training in the industry, it is not surprising that the industry has come to depend more on formal schooling in which the student, or the student's creditors, must bear the up-front costs.

In practice, therefore, formal training efforts within the firm are usually limited to teaching workers the procedures and skills particular to the individual restaurant. Other than that, skill acquisition is left to the initiative of individuals and the interest that skilled workers might have in teaching. The result is a haphazard and uncertain process.

Therefore, when compared to mobility opportunities in large firms with formal job ladders for initially unskilled workers, such opportunities in small firms often suffer due to initially low pay, higher foregone earnings, and the uncertainties inherent in the necessity to switch firms in order to advance the skill accumulation process. In these circumstances, the worker's personal network of friends and contacts within the industry are of central importance in the mobility process. The wider the worker's contacts within the industry, the higher the probability that he or she will be able to move successfully through the variety of jobs and firms that will allow the acquisition of appropriate skills. Personal networks are even more important when this factor is linked to the central role networks play in the hiring process.

To be sure, there are large restaurant corporations that establish job ladders for unskilled workers. One large food-service corporation in New York operates over twenty restaurants and eating places in one location. Many of the restaurants share facilities such as prep-kitchens. The company employs over 1,000 workers, and they often move among units as they learn new skills and take on new responsibilities. Because of the diversity of operations, the wide variety of required skills, and the physical concentration of the business, the management has developed a highly articulated internal labor market that provides opportunities for advancement. Nevertheless, some gaps in the ladders remain. Most of the skilled cooks require formal training; therefore, there is a limit above which unskilled kitchen workers cannot rise. The most active ladders seem to be in the dining rooms where middle-class, often college-educated waiters frequently move into management jobs.

The employment structure of this firm, however, contrasts with the structure of most large restaurant corporations. Instead of having a dense and diverse job structure concentrated in one place, they usually have a thin job structure with few distinct occupations and only simple skill requirements spread out in many small outlets. Paradoxically, the rule in this industry is that those firms such as the fast-food chains that are large enough to be able to establish formal training programs tend to have job structures that minimize the need for nonmanagerial skills. As a result, the formal training that these firms provide is for managers. And like management trainees elsewhere, the students are not unskilled workers with little education and are rarely individuals who have worked their way up through the firm's production jobs. Rather, they are hired from outside the firm and usually have some college education if not bachelor's degrees.

Immigrant Workers
and the Immigration Process

As a result of a close look at the restaurant industry, the stereotype of the unskilled immigrant quickly fades. To be sure, there are many immigrant dishwashers, but the foreign born are also overrepresented among cooks and, as shall be seen in the next chapter, among restaurant owners. The low-skilled jobs in the full-service restaurants in which so many immigrants find work are positions best filled by stable workers willing to work long hours and odd shifts. The higher-level positions in which immigrants are concentrated in this sector depend fundamentally on an uncertain and haphazard skill-acquisition process built around informal networks and relationships. Other studies reveal similar patterns in other industries.[24] The occupational and industrial distributions of the foreign born are also consistent with the assertion that immigrants tend to be concentrated in skilled and unskilled jobs characterized by informal training and employment processes.[25]

What is the explanation of this pattern? We begin with the uncontroversial thesis that many immigrants arrive with few skills. People who have accumulated skills in their home countries find that these skills have little application in the United States; thus there is a characteristic downward mobility of immigrants in the first years after their arrival.[26] Furthermore, as a result of low skills, language deficiencies, inappropriate credentials, and discrimination, immigrants have more limited access, compared to natives, to long-term stable jobs in the public sector or in large firms that have well-organized employment and promotion processes.

These factors tend to channel immigrants into low-skilled jobs and low-wage industries; traits of the immigration process itself reinforce this tendency and indeed further differentiate immigrants from natives. Traditionally, immigration has been conceived as a one-step process in which immigrants leave their home countries to settle permanently in a receiving society. Michael Piore argued that this view of the immigration process is wrong. He stated that "the typical migrant *plans* to spend only a short-time in the industrial area; he then expects to return home. *Staying* represents a change of plans."[27] Migrants come to industrial countries to accumulate savings and remittances to be spent at home. Typically these expenditures include the purchase of land, livestock, store or small business, or a taxi or other vehicle.[28] Thus the migration process can be viewed in investment terms. The investment costs include transportation, living expenses in the new country, and the difficulties associated with being away from home; the returns include the savings.

Several implications with respect to immigrant labor market behavior flow from this temporary perspective. One implication affects the comparison between the jobs in the home and those in the receiving economies. For most immigrants, even the worst jobs in the United States correspond to jobs at least in the middle of the employment hierarchy in the home country. To the extent that immigrants continue to define themselves in terms of their home economies and societies, it is these worse jobs to which they compare their opportunities in the U.S. labor market. Second, because their stay is temporary, they are willing to work long hours under unpleasant conditions because these factors will have to be endured for only a short period. Finally, Piore particularly emphasizes the impact of this temporary perspective on the association between the willingness of immigrants to take a particular type of job and the status, as it is defined by the receiving society, associated with that job. Thus he argues that

> To the considerable extent that the job, and the work that it entails, serves itself to define our social and personal selves, there are decided limits upon what we feel willing and able to do simply to earn money. . . . To a certain extent, attitudes toward work and the acceptability of certain work roles are uniform throughout a society: There are certain jobs that everybody views as humiliating and degrading; other careers that carry a kind of prestige that dignifies anyone who follows them, in their eyes and those of others.

> The social role of the job itself limits considerably the degree to which people will respond to economic incentives. . . . To understand labor—market behavior, in this view, one must concentrate . . . on the process through which people develop the self-conceptions and social orientations that determine their job choices.

> However valid this view—and I personally think it has considerable merit—it does not apply to the labor market for *temporary* immigrants. The temporary character of the migration flow appears to create a sharp distinction between work, on the one hand, and the social identity of the worker, on the other. The individual's social identity is located in the place of origin, the home community. The migration to the industrial community and the work performed there is purely instrumental: a means to gather income, income that can be taken back to his or her home community and used to fulfill or enhance his or her role within *that* social structure. From the perspective of the immigrant, the work is essentially asocial: It is purely a means to an end.[29]

Piore goes on to present examples of migrants who are willing to hold particular jobs only because the migrants are removed from their primary social settings. As one Puerto Rican stated, "If I am going to do that sort of work I'd rather do it over there [on the mainland]. Then, I can come home and be myself."[30] Based on the implications of the migrant's temporary perspective, Piore concludes that migrants are willing to take jobs "that the native labor force refuses to accept."[31]

Piore argues that these factors flow from the immigrants' temporary perspective. But many of the factors that shape the labor supply of temporary migrants also influence the employment of immigrants with a longer-term perspective.

The permanent immigrants' willingness to take low-quality employment is conditioned, as it is for temporary migrants, by their incomplete integration into the social and economic system that establishes these jobs as low-paid, low-status positions. Of course, as with temporary migrants, low-quality jobs in the receiving society provide higher incomes than would be available at home. Furthermore, although the plan to return to the home country weakens the process of social integration, even without such a plan, integration takes time. At least at first, secondary-sector jobs do not look so bad socially or economically to immigrants as they do to native-born workers.

Furthermore, although immigrants who plan to stay may be more concerned with finding career employment than temporary immigrants are, the former also experience the transition characteristics of the immigration process. Their immediate postarrival employment can be purely instrumental—a limited period of long hours of low-paid work that allows them to establish themselves, bring over their families, perhaps open their own small businesses, or take advantage of other opportunities that become available once they make contacts.

The characteristics that have been considered so far (low skill levels; restricted alternatives; the willingness to work enthusiastically long hours at jobs unacceptable to many natives; an investment orientation that discounts current hardships for future goals) are more than adequate to explain why immigrants are concentrated in low-quality employment. But the argument in the previous chapter suggests that immigrants, even those arriving with few skills, also fill skilled positions under certain conditions. The explanation for this lies in the dynamics of the settlement process as well as in the initial conditions under which the newcomers immigrate.

The jobs the immigrants hold initially, though unskilled, are in a wide variety of firms and enterprises. Thus newcomers are employed as entry-level workers in large ranches and factories as well as in tiny bodegas. Nevertheless, low-wage, unstable employment is associated with small firms, low capitalization, and competitive markets. Indeed, many recently arrived immigrants meet the labor needs of restaurants, garment factories, retail outlets, and other establishments with small work forces. Such firms also rely, more than large bureaucratized establishments, on informal and haphazard procedures for recruitment, training, and promotion.

Furthermore, one implication of the investment orientation and the temporary perspective of the early periods of immigration is that recent immigrants are not only willing to work long workweeks but often seek jobs that will give them the opportunity to work extra hours. Long workweeks not only maximize income and therefore potential savings, but they also minimize the cost of the "investment" by discouraging consumption. Thus many restaurant employers reported that their immigrant employees often worked sixty hours a week. Census data also show that immigrant restaurant workers are more likely than natives to work over forty hours.[32]

During the settlement process, immigrants may begin to lose the orientation and perspective that made initial employment in low-status jobs and industries look good. Nevertheless, their initial location in industries characterized by small firms and their intensive employment there result in the acquisition of particular skills, experience, and contacts. These in turn create strong incentives to stay in those industries and to take advantage of whatever opportunities for economic mobility are available even though those opportunities may look unattractive from the viewpoint of workers outside of the industry who would have to start in the lowest-level jobs.

Family and ethnic ties in the immigrant community are additional factors that channel immigrants into particular industries and help them to acquire skills there. The legal framework that shapes immigration to the United States selects individuals who are integrated into social networks. Family relationships are the primary basis on which claims for permanent resident status are made, and friendship and family ties enhance the possibilities for arrival and employment as an undocumented alien.

Many labor market studies, including the restaurant case study, demonstrate the central role played by informal networks in hiring and job search. The more extensive an individual's contacts, the more likely it is that he or she will know about job openings and the more people there will be who can serve as sponsors or references for that individual. But as the restaurant case study suggests, some types of production processes rely on informal network hiring more than others. Other things being equal, groups with strong networks are more likely to be concentrated in these jobs. Moreover, once a group is established in such a labor market niche, continued reliance on network hiring serves as a barrier to the entrance of other groups.

There is now extensive theoretical literature on the role of networks in job finding.[33] Much of this work emphasizes the distinction, first discussed by Mark Granovetter, between strong ties, which link friends and family, and weak ties, which link acquaintances. Granovetter views the world as a collection of "densely knit clumps of social structure."[34] The individuals in one clump share strong ties, but each group member also has acquaintances who are themselves members of a separate clump. It is the weak ties that serve as bridges between different closely knit groups and are therefore a vital source of information. But these ties obviously will be more useful if they provide information that can broaden opportunities. Thus weak ties improve occupational status only when they serve as a bridge to higher-status individuals.[35]

How do these distinctions apply to the immigrants' use of personal networks? First, it has been argued that for temporary immigrants and at least initially for permanent immigrants, long-term occupational mobility is not a central goal. Therefore in the short term, even low-status contacts can help immigrant workers meet their goals. But from a longer-term perspective, the usefulness of contacts depends on the extent to which immigrant networks bridge social distance. Although he does not address this question directly, Piore implies that networks do accomplish this. He states that "the middle class migrants create the institutional structure required to link the countryside of their own country with the industrialized nation abroad."[36] The notion of "chain migrants" described in numerous case studies, which is defined as "that movement in which migrants learn of opportunities, are provided with transportation, and have initial accommodation and employment arranged by means of primary social relationships with previous migrants,"[37] suggests that strong or weak, the ties of many immigrants provide useful information.

Finally, the labor processes in the volatile less-institutionalized industries in which immigrants start out are in many ways similar to those processes in the labor markets of the sending countries. In the past ten years there has been an increased interest in the informal sector of urban labor markets of the developing countries.[38] These informal sectors are dominated by petty entrepreneurs, artisans, and traders. Labor market studies in less-developed countries indicate that in many countries informal sectors account for over 50 percent of urban employment.[39] Moreover, contemporary immigrants are not drawn from the lowest rural strata of the sending countries but rather from the urban lower and middle classes—precisely the individuals who are likely to have had experience in the informal sectors of their home countries.

Several factors, therefore, come together to channel recent immigrants into industries dominated by small firms using informal production and labor processes. The immigrants' initial low skill levels, lingering identification with the home economy and culture, premigration experiences, the informal sectors in their home countries, and the social networks that help them migrate in the first place make them well adapted for the particular labor needs of small, marginal firms. The gradual process of adaptation and identification with the receiving country, the experience accumulated during the early phase of residence, and once again, networks that brought the immigrants and that developed after arrival fit well with the training processes in these industries and thereby channel immigrants into the higher-level jobs. The next chapter will extend this argument to show how it helps explain the propensity of immigrants for self-employment and their relative success in entrepreneurship.

Notes

1. See note 9 in Chapter 1 for a comparison of the occupational distribution of immigrant and native workers. The same census, *Public Use Microdata Samples*, referred to in that note indicates that in New York City 9.7 percent of the employed natives and 15.7 percent of the foreign born (almost 20 percent of those arriving after 1974) worked in nondurable manufacturing in 1980. Twelve percent of the natives worked in retail trade and 2.6 percent in personal services. During the same year, 16 percent of the foreign born were employed in retail trade and 5.7 percent in personal services. Once again, the differences were greater for more recent immigrants.

2. Tony Lawson, "Paternalism and Labour Market Segmentation Theory," in Frank Wilkinson, ed., *The Dynamics of Labor Market Segmentation* (London: Academic Press, 1981), p. 48.

3. Max Weber, *The Theory of Social and Economic Organization* (New York, N.Y.: Free Press, 1947), p. 341.

4. The following quotation by John Stuart Mill is an explicit and clear statement of this point of view: "The lot of the poor, in all things which affect them collectively, should be regulated *for* them, not *by* them. They should not be required or encouraged to think for themselves, or give to their own reflection or forecast an influential voice in the determination of their destiny. It is the duty of the higher classes to think for them, and to take the responsibility of their lot, as the commander and officers of an army take that of the soldiers composing it. This function the higher classes should prepare themselves to perform conscientiously, and their whole demeanor should impress the poor with a reliance on it, in order that, while yielding passive and

active obedience to the rules prescribed for them, they may resign themselves in all other respects to a trustful *insouciance,* and repose under the shadow of their protectors. The relation between rich and poor should be only partially authoritative; it should be amiable, moral, and sentimental; affectionate tutelage on the one side, respectful and grateful deference on the other." Quoted in Reinhard Bendix, *Work and Authority in Industry* (Berkeley, Cal.: University of California Press, 1956), p. 47, and in Howard Newby, "Paternalism and Capitalism," in Richard Scase, ed., *Industrial Society: Class, Cleavage and Control* (New York, N.Y.: St. Martins Press, 1977).

5. Bendix, 1956.

6. Bendix (1956, p. 51) states that "The traditional approach emphasized the arbitrary will of the master, whose judgment of what was good for his workers was absolute, whose interest, convenience, and petty selfishness frequently prevailed. It required not only a humane regard for the workers but an iron self-discipline and sense for business organization if the despotism implied by the traditional approach was to be benevolent rather than tyrannical."

7. See, for example, Suzanne Berger and Michael Piore, *Dualism and Discontinuity in Industrial Societies* (New York, N.Y.: Cambridge University Press, 1980).

8. Richard Edwards, *Contested Terrain: The Transformation of the Workplace in the Twentieth Century* (New York, N.Y.: Basic Books, Inc., 1979).

9. Edwards, 1979, p. 166.

10. Peter Doeringer and Michael Piore, *Internal Labor Markets and Manpower Analysis* (Lexington, Mass.: Lexington Books, 1971).

11. Robert Buchele, "Jobs and Workers: A Labor Market Segmentation Perspective on the Work Experience of Middle-Aged Men" (PhD dissertation, Economics Department, Harvard University, 1975); and Sam Rosenberg, "A Survey of Empirical Work on Labor Market Segmentation" (Davis, Cal.: University of California, 1979), unpublished.

12. Lawson, 1981; and Peter B. Doeringer, "Internal Labor Markets and Paternalism in Rural Areas," in *Internal Labor Markets* (Cambridge, Mass.: MIT Press, 1984).

13. Lawson, 1981.

14. Doeringer, 1984.

15. The concept of implicit contracts has come to play an increasingly central role in the mainstream economic understanding of labor markets, although it borrows a great deal from the research of institutionalists. Most of the work on implicit contracts is concerned with macro movements of wages and employment. Consequently, the research is designed to explore what the macro implications would be if such agreements did exist. Other research has more clearly addressed the problem of why implicit contracts come about in the first place. See Oliver O. Williamson, Michael L. Wachter, and Jeffrey E. Harris, "Understanding the Employment Relation: The Analysis of Idiosyncratic Exchange," *The Bell Journal of Economics* 6 (Spring 1975): 250–280; Doeringer and Piore, 1971; and George Akerloff, "Gift Exchange and Efficiency Wage Theory," *American Economic Review* 74 (May 1984): 79–83. But the internal labor market and implicit contract literature focuses at least

implicitly on large firms. In this respect, it is interesting that although Doeringer and Piore as well as Akerloff refer to Weberian bureaucratic authority, traditional authority is not considered. Indeed, according to the dual labor market model, in the secondary sector, where small firm size might promote the use of paternalism, the labor market is assumed to conform to the standard competitive model. Hansen makes an interesting attempt to apply the theory of internal labor markets to the informal sector in developing countries where the firms are indeed small. See Bent Hansen, "LDC Labor Markets: Applications of Internal Labor Market Theory," *Industrial Relations* 22 (Spring 1983): 238–260.

16. Research has also confirmed the relationships between low turnover and the use of current employees as informal recruiters. See Martin Gammon, "Sources of Referral and Employee Turnover," *Journal of Applied Psychology* (1971): 226; and Joseph Ullman, "Interfirm Differences in the Cost of Search for Clerical Workers," *Journal of Business* (April 1968): 53.

17. Albert Rees, "Information Networks in Labor Markets," *American Economic Review* 56 (May 1966): 559–566; David Stevens, "A Reexamination of What is Known About Jobseeking Behavior in the United States," in Eli Ginzberg, ed., *Labor Market Intermediaries* (Washington, D.C.: National Commission for Manpower Policy, 1978); and Richard Toikka, "The Economics of Information: Labor Market Aspects," *Swedish Journal of Economics* (March 1974).

18. Andrew Yarrow, "More Slices in the Food-Service Pie," in "National Employment Report, Careers '85," *New York Times* (October 14, 1984): 27.

19. Yarrow, 1984, p. 27.

20. According to the job descriptions in the questionnaire for the New York Department of Labor wage survey, a general cook "prepares, seasons, and cooks, by appropriate method, soups, meats, vegetables, desserts, and other foodstuffs, such as sauces, gravies, and salads."

21. Excludes shift differentials, overtime premiums, holiday pay, and value of perquisites.

22. Walter Fogel, "Occupational Earnings: Market and Institutional Influences," *Industrial and Labor Relations Review* 33 (October 1979): 24–35.

23. David Taylor and Michael Piore also found that economic mobility in the restaurant industry required movement among restaurants. David Taylor and Michael Piore, "Federal Training Programs for Dispersed Employment Occupations," Working Paper Number 42 (Cambridge, Mass.: Department of Economics, Massachusetts Institute of Technology, 1968).

24. Carmenza Gallo, "The Construction Industry in New York City: Immigrants and Black Entrepreneurs," Working Paper (New York, N.Y.: Columbia University, Conservation of Human Resources, 1983); and Roger Waldinger, *Through the Eye of the Needle: Immigrant Enterprise in New York's Garment Trades* (New York, N.Y.: New York University Press, 1986).

25. See note 9 in Chapter 1 and note 1 in this chapter.

26. Barry R. Chiswick, "The Effect of Americanization on the Earnings of Foreign-Born Men," *Journal of Political Economy* 86 (October 1978): 897–921.

27. Michael Piore, *Birds of Passage: Migrant Labor and Industrial Societies* (New York, N.Y.: Cambridge University Press, 1979), p. 51.

28. Piore, 1979, p. 56.

29. Piore, 1979, pp. 53–54.

30. Piore, 1979, p. 54.

31. Piore, 1979, p. 3.

32. In New York City, 32 percent of the male foreign-born compared to 21 percent of the male native-born restaurant workers reported that during 1979 they normally worked more than forty hours a week. *Census of Population: 1980, Public Use Microdata Samples.*

33. A bibliography as well as recent contributions by many of the leading scholars in the field can be found in Peter V. Marsden and Nan Lin, eds., *Social Structure and Network Analysis* (Beverly Hills, Cal.: Sage Publications, 1982).

34. Mark S. Granovetter, "The Strength of Weak Ties: A Network Theory Revisited," in Marsden and Lin, 1982, p. 106.

35. Nan Lin, N.W.M. Ensel, and J. C. Vaughn, "Social Resources and Strength of Ties: Structural Factors in Occupational Status Attainment," *American Sociological Review* 46 (1981): 393–405.

36. Piore, 1979, p. 140.

37. John S. MacDonald and Beatrice D. MacDonald, "Chain Migration, Ethnic Neighborhood Formation and Social Network," in Charles Tilly, ed., *An Urban World* (Boston, Mass.: Little, Brown, 1974), p. 227.

38. An early discussion of the informal sector can be found in International Labor Organization, *Employment, Incomes and Equality: A Strategy for Increasing Productive Employment in Kenya* (Geneva: ILO, 1972). A useful review is included in Dipak Mazumdar, "The Urban Informal Sector," *World Development* 4 (August 1976): 655–679. See also "Third World Migration and Urbanization: A Symposium," *Economic Development and Cultural Change* (April 1982).

39. Mazumdar, 1976.

3

Immigrant Owners

The hustling immigrant entrepreneur holds an established position in the history and mythology of U.S. society. Indeed, a casual look at the ethnicity of the retail merchants in many of the nation's largest cities indicates that once again many immigrants are establishing small businesses. Almost every block in New York City has a Korean greengrocery or an Indian or Pakistani newsstand;[1] and Israeli taxi owners/drivers are a common sight.[2] Immigrants are also opening businesses in less visible locations: Dominicans and Chinese own garment shops while West Indians and Hispanics work as construction contractors.[3]

It is through immigrant ownership that the importance of immigrant employment in the restaurant industry appears most obvious to patrons. In the other subsectors of the restaurant industry, immigrants tend to be concentrated in kitchen occupations out of the public sight. The immigrant concentration among the self-employed is reflected in the restaurant industry. Sixty-five percent of the restaurants in the 1981 telephone survey conducted for this study were owned by first-generation immigrants.[4] These restaurants probably accounted for about 40 percent of the restaurant market in New York City. As early as 1970, 43 percent of all the self-employed in the industry in the city were first-generation immigrants, and by 1980, this figure had risen to 60 percent.[5]

In this chapter the distinctive characteristics of the immigrant sector of the restaurant industry are described. Building on the argument developed in Chapter 2, the chapter then considers why immigrants are concentrated among the self-employed and closes with a discussion of the garment industry as an additional example.

The Immigrant Sector

There are many relatively expensive immigrant-owned restaurants, but the immigrant sector's comparative advantage appears to lie primarily at the lower-priced end of the market. Table 3.1 presents the distribution of restaurants in the 1981 survey by price and nativity of owner. Of the ninety-seven restaurants in the sample with average checks below $8, only thirty-one were not owned by immigrants. A comparison between low-priced immigrant-owned and native-owned restaurants in the survey indicates that the two types of restaurants, which use different technologies, compete in the low-priced segment of the market.

Chain outlets were much more important in the native-owned sectors. Thirteen of the thirty-one units were parts of chains. Of the remaining eighteen, five were relatively expensive intermediate sector restaurants (average check per person over $6) that competed with full-service or expensive immigrant restaurants, three were owned by second-generation immigrants who either had ties to their immigrant communities or operated with family members exclusively, and one was owned by a Puerto Rican. The inexpensive segment of the industry in New York is therefore characterized by competition among native-owned chain outlets and immigrant-owned independent restaurants. Independent ownership of low-priced restaurants in New York is primarily an immigrant phenomenon.

The production process in immigrant restaurants remains traditional. Some have taken advantage of technological changes, but even in moderately priced immigrant restaurants, cooking skills have not been entirely eliminated. Many low-priced establishments, such as modest Chinese restaurants, have extensive menus that prevent the standardization and bulk ordering of pre-prepared foods that offer the largest savings. Because of these factors, the production process in the immigrant sector is not based on the use of workers primarily as

TABLE 3.1
Restaurants Surveyed, by Price Range and Nativity of Owner,
New York City, 1981

Ownership	Less Than $8 per Meal	More Than $8 per Meal	Total
Native-born	31	33	64
Immigrant	66	26	92
Total	97	59	156

Source: Data collected by the author in 1981.

machine tenders and sales clerks as it is in the fast-food sector. Because cooking and entrepreneurial skills are required and because most of these skills are learned on the job, the immigrant sector depends on full-time, long-term workers. When part-time workers are used, they are often friends of the owner or family members.

The production process of the immigrant sector is therefore similar to the process that predominates in the full-service sector. Nevertheless, among the four sectors, immigrant-owned restaurants have been most resistant to the main trends that have swept the industry. In contrast to managers of fast-food restaurants, immigrant and native-born full-service owners depend on the availability of both unskilled and skilled restaurant workers who are attached to the industry. And immigrant restaurants, even more than full-service establishments, continue to depend on informally trained cooks and managers. Moreover, despite many similarities between the labor processes in the immigrant and full-service sectors, important differences remain.

The mobilization of familial, ethnic, and social ties within the immigrant community is a fundamental difference between the labor processes of the immigrant and full-service sectors. Many immigrant restaurants, in fact, operate without paid employees. When workers are needed, restaurateurs in this sector, with some exceptions, hire immigrants exclusively and when possible, from their own home countries. In cases in which the work force extends beyond the family to other immigrants, the owners and employees often accept a set of obligations that are characteristic of a family enterprise. Indeed, in the immigrant business, the paternalistic employment system that is used in the full-service sector is even more important.

In the full-service sector, the system of reciprocal but implicit obligations is wedded to outside social relationships primarily through reliance on network hiring. On the one hand, the owner attempts to provide stable employment as well as personal favors and discretionary benefits and to give preference to the family and friends of current employees. On the other hand, the workers exhibit dependable and stable behavior, help the employer recruit replacements when needed, and participate in the supervision and integration of new workers. Thus the owner taps an existing network through the use of representatives or key workers.

In the immigrant firm, the owner can draw on his own network without the need of intermediation. This strengthens the ties between owner and worker and obscures the inherent conflicts of an authoritarian relationship. The greater the knowledge about the employee, the stronger the owner's control. Moreover, it reduces the chance, present in the full-service sector (where networks are imported and operated through intermediaries) that the network will engage in solidaristic behavior against the owner. As will be shown, however, the immigrant owner's obligations appear to be more extensive. Furthermore, often the owners themselves have worked their way up through lower-level restaurant occupations and at least have more understanding than native owners of the problems employees encounter, although, to be sure, this is no guarantee that the owners will treat workers benevolently. In any case, since both owner and worker are experiencing the process of immigration, it is not surprising that the owner's role involves dynamic aspects such as training and economic mobility in contrast to the more static role played by full-service owners. Although the obligations may not always be in the short-term interest of one or both of the parties, they are understood to be mutually advantageous within the broader context of the process of immigration and settlement.

One effect of this is that paternalism in this sector is used in restaurants competing in the low-priced segments of the market. Among native-owned establishments, paternalism is found primarily in units serving the expensive end of the market. In the rest of this section, the implications of this production process both for the competitive position of the immigrant sector as well as for the immigrant worker will be examined in more detail.

Advantages for Immigrants
Working in the Sector

As I have pointed out, the personnel practices in immigrant restaurants tend to be paternalistic, as they are in the full-service sector. Thus the owner often allows some flexibility in scheduling for extraordinary events or for visits to the home country, layoffs are avoided during seasonal fluctuations, and bonuses and informal financial assistance are sometimes provided at the discretion of the owner.

To be sure, the paternalistic employment process is often abused. In the survey, examples were found in which newly arrived undocumented Chinese immigrants were paid only carfare and meals. Immigrants who do not speak English and have no skills are legally vulnerable and are easily exploited. Under any circumstances, unskilled jobs in immigrant restaurants offer long hours at low pay. Nevertheless, immigrant workers in the sector do enjoy advantages that are less available in other sectors. One such advantage involves adjustments to the U.S. economy and society during the early stages of immigration.

At the least, the ethnic firm provides a linguistically and culturally familiar environment for recent arrivals. Owners and coworkers help out with various social and legal problems, and immigrant owners sometimes help with status adjustment. One manager interviewed for this study said that after his arrival on a tourist visa, he found a job as a dishwasher in a restaurant owned by a countryman who helped him get his green card by claiming that he was a skilled chef. Some establishments are informal way stations where recent immigrants who know friends or relatives of the owners can earn a little money and make contacts while looking for a longer-term job. Several immigrants said that their employment experience in immigrant establishments had helped them in their postarrival adjustment.

The long workweeks in many ethnic restaurants are also an advantage for some immigrants. Workers who are accumulating savings or sending home remittances want to maximize their work hours and minimize their consumption expenditures. Working ten hours a day in a restaurant leaves little time to spend money. These workers usually receive two free meals a day, which further reduces their expenditures. Often managers in other sectors may be less willing to employ workers for long workweeks because of overtime premiums. In the immigrant sector, these premiums are often ignored.

Perhaps the most important advantage available to workers in immigrant restaurants is the opportunity to learn both cooking and entrepreneurial skills. The structure of the restaurant industry militates against the development of organized skill-acquisition processes by creating incentives for owners to avoid training costs. The more complicated relationships in the immigrant sector help to create mechanisms and incentives to promote training, but they are generally absent in the other sectors of the restaurant industry. In most restaurants, workers are unlikely to learn skills in return for their initial low-paid work. In the immigrant sector, this trade-off is more often understood to be part of the owner's role. Many immigrant owners said that they expect their workers to learn skills and encourage them to do so. Native-born owners were much less likely to emphasize their training roles, often stating that they did not have time to train.

Immigrant owners are also less likely to discriminate against other immigrants in hiring for particular occupations. Whereas many native-owned restaurants hire few if any immigrants as managers or waiters, most of these jobs are held by immigrants in the immigrant sector. These opportunities for immigrants influence the expectations and incentives of low-level employees in this sector, but they also affect the incentives of immigrants employed in the other sectors who believe that they have some chance to move into the better occupations in the immigrant sector. This contrasts with the situation of blacks, who are also often barred from front-of-the-house jobs but have no sector of their own where they would have easier access to better opportunities.

The thesis that immigrant workers benefit from employment in this sector is consistent with the conclusions of a study by Kenneth Wilson and Alejandro Portes who found that Cuban employment in secondary-sector firms not owned by Cubans was associated with "less income satisfaction, less occupational prestige and less willingness to come to the United States if the decision had to be taken again" than employment in Cuban-owned firms.[6] Wilson and Portes conclude that "this line of reasoning suggests that the low-wage labor of immigrant workers is what permits survival and expansion of enclave enterprises which, in turn, open new opportunities for economic advancement."[7]

A study of Macedonian self-employment in the restaurant industry in Toronto also found that immigrants employed in restaurants owned by their countrymen enjoyed advantages. As a dishwasher in a Macedonian-owned restaurant, "a newcomer might earn less than he could in a factory or a sawmill, but he could enjoy the company and support of people who spoke his language and shared his values. More important, he could, in the long term, expect to move up the restaurant hierarchy into self-employment."[8]

Entrepreneurship

Indeed the opportunity for entrepreneurship in the immigrant sector is one of the most important advantages offered the immigrant worker as well as one of the central factors that perpetuates and strengthens the sector's market position. Despite the growth of chains, the restaurant industry still retains opportunities for small-scale entrepreneurs. In 1982, the average number of employees per establishment with a payroll in the industry was 14.9, although the median was between seven and nine. Forty-six percent had fewer than seven employees (see Table 3.2). These data overstate the size of restaurants because they exclude establishments with no payroll. Although data on average capital costs are not available, sales data suggest that a small restaurant employing five or six workers requires an initial capital investment of well under $50,000 (1987 dollars) and that a small restaurant operated only by owners and family members (13.1 percent of all establishments in the industry had no payroll) requires an initial investment of about $25,000.[9] Therefore initial investments for at least a significant minority of the industry's firms can be met by the savings and credit that can be accumulated by an

TABLE 3.2
Size Distribution, U.S. Eating and Drinking Places, 1982

Paid Employees, Year-round Establishments	Number	Percentage	Sales[a]	Percentage
Total	288,315	100.0	$93,907,830	100.0
0[b]	14,057	4.9	1,284,272	1.4
1	27,204	9.4	1,430,081	1.5
2	25,151	8.7	1,830,854	1.9
3–4	38,708	13.4	3,862,165	4.1
5–6	26,319	9.1	3,578,402	3.8
7–9	28,707	10.0	5,275,414	5.6
10–14	36,307	12.6	9,841,796	10.5
15–19	21,641	7.5	7,673,218	8.2
20–49	53,928	18.7	34,159,143	36.4
50–99	13,966	4.8	18,233,181	19.4
100 or more	2,327	0.8	6,739,304	7.2

[a]Sales in thousands of dollars.
[b]Had no employees at date of survey.

Source: U.S. Bureau of the Census, *Census of Retail Trade: 1982, Industry Series, Establishment and Firm Size*, RC 82-I-1 (Washington, D.C.: GPO), table 2.

individual or a small group of friends or relatives even if they start with no assets and without advanced skills.

The experience of many immigrant owners interviewed for this study illustrates this pattern of initial low-level employment, followed by accumulation of skills and savings, and eventual entry into business with relatively small amounts of capital.   The following cases are examples:

The owner of a small Colombian restaurant in Queens has been in the country for nine years. She first started working as a dishwasher in a Colombian restaurant. At the time she did not have a green card. A few months after she started, the cook left and she was promoted. She learned the skills with the help of her boss and some of her customers. After three years, she found a job in a plastics factory at higher pay. Two-and-a-half years later, her old employer asked her to come back at a higher wage. She returned as the cook with an assistant. Two years later, she used her savings and a bank loan to open the restaurant. Interestingly, she asked permission of her old employer to solicit customers for her new place. He agreed.

The owner of two Greek diners in Manhattan jumped ship in Philadelphia in 1956 when he was eighteen and worked as a dishwasher until he was apprehended by the Immigration and Naturalization Service in 1958 and was required to ship out on another freighter. He jumped ship again, and this time got his green card in 1959 when he married a U.S. citizen. By 1960, he had saved enough money to open a small diner of his own.

The manager of a large Chinese restaurant in Chinatown arrived eleven years ago from Hong Kong when he was twenty years old. His parents were "regular working people." He wanted to study when he arrived, but did not have the money, so he looked for work in restaurants. His first job was in a Chinese restaurant in the Bronx where he received no pay. After one week he left and has since worked in many Chinese restaurants. He has now saved enough to look for partners to open a restaurant. He says that several partners are required because they need about $50,000 to start.

The owner of an Ecuadorian restaurant in Queens has been in the United States for about ten years. In Ecuador he had worked with his father in a small business. When he first arrived, he worked in factories for a few months. Then he got a job as a dishwasher at Nathan's. After that he worked for about seven years in an expensive Spanish restaurant in Manhattan, starting out as a dishwasher, then cook's helper and second cook. Three years ago, he bought this restaurant with personal savings and a purchase money mortgage from the previous owner. He said that he made more money as a waiter in fewer hours with fewer headaches but that he preferred to be his own boss.

The owner of another Greek diner arrived in 1958 and got a job at a Greek hot-dog stand in the Greyhound Bus Terminal. He and his boss became partners at an ice-cream stand, first in Harlem and then on 12th Street. In 1963, they each put up $4,000 to buy the present restaurant. They eventually paid the former owner $28,000.

Of course, not all immigrants worked their way up from the bottom:

A Korean owner of a cafeteria serving Italian food has been in the United States for four years. In Korea, he worked for an airline. He is a college graduate. He came to the United States because there is no retirement insurance in Korea and because the "political situation was unstable." When he arrived, he bought a stationery store. Three months ago he bought the restaurant from a Greek who went back to Greece. He depends heavily on the Greek cook because the Korean has no restaurant experience.

Overall, of the twenty-nine immigrant owners and managers who provided information on their employment background, all but four worked as employees in local restaurants before moving to their present positions. Another worked only three months before buying a restaurant. Four had owned restaurants in their home countries, but only one of them had been able to purchase a restaurant without having to work up through other restaurants in New York. Two had had experience in restaurants as employees before they left their home countries. Of the twenty-nine, nineteen had arrived without having worked in restaurants in any capacity.

The results of the survey suggest that capital as well as skills were acquired in the United States, not in the home country. Of the twenty immigrant respondents who discussed their financial sources, all had used personal savings, but only two had used savings amassed before emigrating. No one reported that he or she had benefited from the type of formally organized rotating credit associations that have received so much attention in the immigration literature. Nevertheless, loans from family and friends play a central role in the informal capital markets that fuel the immigrant sector. Fourteen of the owners had borrowed money either from their families or from the previous owners of their restaurants. Suppliers are also sources of credit in the early stages. Only six reported that they received loans from banks or from the Small Business Administration for initial investment and start-up costs, although others had acquired credit from financial institutions for expansion sometime after the restaurant had been established; and some Greek and Chinese owners had acquired loans to purchase their restaurants after they had already established other restaurants with informal financing.

The pooling of resources in partnerships is another means of accumulating capital. Of the thirty-one immigrant owners who reported the ownership organization of their establishments, only ten had started their businesses as the sole owner. Nine other restaurants were owned jointly by family members. Four of these nine were owned by brothers living separately; the other five were owned by husband and wife or parents and children. Twelve were organized in partnerships among unrelated individuals. Partnerships are particularly important among the Chinese. One restaurant in the survey was owned by ten partners and another by fifteen.

Available data cannot reveal the probability that a young immigrant dishwasher will be successful in establishing his or her own restaurant, but the ratio of immigrant owners to immigrant workers gives some indication. A high ratio indicates that there are few entrepreneurial opportunities for immigrants. Within the immigrant sector the ratio is less than 5 to 1. The ratio of all immigrant restaurant workers to immigrant owners is less than 10 to 1.[10] To be sure, the ratio of owners to workers at a given time does not reflect the total number of workers who move through the industry. However, there are also many immigrant workers—older workers, moonlighters, some women, temporary migrants—who are not candidates for ownership and thereby increase the relative availability of ownership slots for those who want them.

Regardless of the actual probability, the ratios suggest that for young immigrant workers who can work long workweeks, the ambition to open their own restaurants is not completely unrealistic. From their viewpoint, the chances of this type of mobility may seem particularly good because many of their countrymen or even relatives who are self-employed started out in unskilled jobs.

Advantages for Owners

As data from the telephone survey indicate, immigrant-owned restaurants are concentrated in the low-priced segment of the market. What allows these restaurants to compete against the highly capitalized fast-food and intermediate sector chains that use advanced technology and modern managerial and organizational practices? One possibility is that immigrant-owned restaurants survive on the demand generated by the immigrant community itself. To be sure, each immigrant neighborhood has restaurants that serve primarily natives from a particular country. Frequently the owners and even the waiters in the restaurants speak little English. Community demand undoubtedly provides a base for an expanding network of restaurants serving the food of particular sending countries. Nevertheless, patrons of the Chinese restaurants in New York's Chinatown, the Indian restaurants on East Sixth Street, the Cuban restaurants on Manhattan's Upper West Side, or ethnic restaurants all over New York City and many other large cities can see that these restaurants serve large numbers of native-born clients. Indeed, the spread of Italian, Chinese, Mexican, and Greek restaurants in cities and towns all over the United States is further indication of the wide demand for ethnic foods.

This suggests another possibility—the demand generated by the variety and uniqueness of ethnic foods. Undoubtedly, a strong demand for ethnic foods would create opportunities for immigrant owners who have a comparative advantage in the preparation of food from their countries. Nevertheless, at the low end of the market, where ethnic restaurants are concentrated, the demand for the products of immigrant-owned restaurants has as much to do with the price as with the palate. The ubiquitous Greek-owned coffee shops that serve primarily hamburgers are the best illustration. Although some owners try to maintain a Greek identity by serving feta cheese on salads, this ethnic touch hardly accounts for their success. In any case, it is worth noting that immigrants are overrepresented in the production of many goods and services that are associated with no ethnic group, suggesting that entrepreneurship among immigrants does not only depend on their comparative advantage in producing ethnic products.

The labor process that predominates in the immigrant sector affords owners cost advantages that strengthen their competitive positions. In particular, these owners enjoy lower labor costs and tighter control over the work process. Many workers in the sector are paid at or below the minimum hourly wage. At the time of the survey, Chinese dishwashers made $650 to $750 a month for workweeks as long as sixty hours; Greek diners paid up to $200 a week for sixty hours, although these wages were often paid in cash and therefore were equivalent to somewhat higher taxed wages, particularly if meals are taken into consideration. This form of tax evasion, which is made easier by the close relationships between owners and workers, is advantageous to both.

Furthermore, in many immigrant restaurants, there seems to be only a weak connection between pay and hours, at least in the short run. Owners interviewed for this study tended to quote weekly or monthly pay instead of hourly wages, even for unskilled workers. It was understood that workers were available for extra hours when needed. Although they sometimes receive bonuses or favors, the extra hours do not necessarily result in more pay. This provides a flexibility that is at least as important an advantage as low hourly wage scales. Violation of overtime provisions in the law is probably more widespread than violation of the base minimum wage. Flexibility is enhanced by the availability of friends and family, many with restaurant experience, who can fill in when necessary. The owner also usually has experience in all of the jobs in the restaurant and can substitute for absent workers or help out when business is brisk. All of these factors save labor costs by allowing the owner to understaff.

Employing workers for extra long workweeks minimizes the total number of employees, an important advantage in a management style that depends on close relationships, which would be impossible to develop with battalions of tenuously attached part-timers with high turnover rates. Underreporting of wages and sales is also less risky when the number of workers is small. Furthermore, if an employee works sixty hours, the employer can report a fraction of actual working hours and still keep a large proportion of the pay off the books.

The traditional relationships in the immigrant sector also tend to discourage unionization and the accompanying work rules and workweek limitations. This barrier to unionization is particularly strong when the workers are closely related to the owner or when the workers themselves hope eventually to move up to ownership. These factors blur the distinction between the interests of the workers and those of the owners. Therefore, of the twenty-four immigrant restaurants surveyed that were not owned by Greeks, not one was organized. Some of the Greek restaurants did have union contracts, but not with the major restaurant and hotel union in New York. These owners were reluctant to discuss their relations with the union and implied that the interests of the workers were not the unions' primary concern. One interviewee stated that his restaurant was organized but that he was the only union member. Another said he had no contact with the union except to send them a check for $300 every month.

Thus owners in the immigrant sector have unusually good initial access to low-priced labor and are able to mobilize it in ways that keep the labor costs down. This of course applies to unskilled workers, but as the argument in Chapter 2 suggests, the nature of the relationships and the motivation that characterize the restaurants in this sector also create an advantageous environment for informal training and skill acquisition. Thus although native owners are reluctant to train, thereby perpetuating the shortages of cooks, immigrant owners are more willing to devote time to training, thereby strengthening the availability of skilled workers.

Furthermore, in the immigrant sector, workers see owners who themselves may have worked their way up from unskilled positions. Thus by making entrepreneurial ambition appear more realistic, incentives are created for young immigrants to acquire skills. To be sure, the industry as a whole benefits from a supply of skilled cooks, but to the extent that skills are specific to particular types of food, the impact is strongest in the immigrant sector.

Low labor costs, flexibility to adjust to hourly and seasonal fluctuations, resistance to unionization, and the avoidance of problems caused by skill shortages are achieved in the fast-food sector by the use of a technology that requires few skills and a labor force of short-term, part-time workers. In contrast, immigrant owners can achieve these same objectives using a traditional labor-intensive technology that requires skills and that operates most efficiently with full-time, long-term workers.

Thus the immigrant sector and its labor process represents a distinctive type of structure for economic opportunity and mobility through the acquisition of food-service and entrepreneurial skills that differs from the structures found increasingly in the full-service sector and among the chains, which depend either on acquisition of formal training or movement through the hierarchy in one firm. In the next section I take a broader look at the forces that channel immigrants into small businesses such as restaurants and result in their concentration among entrepreneurs.

The Origins of Immigrant Entrepreneurship

Successful operation of a small business has several requirements: (1) market and technological conditions must exist that will allow a small business to flourish; (2) the potential entrepreneur must have an orientation toward small business activity and the hard work and high risk involved; (3) a means of accumulating start-up captial must exist; (4) small businesses must have contact with suppliers, customers, and others involved in the industry or business; (5) the entrepreneur must be able to learn the required skills; and (6) the entrepreneur must have access to a low-cost labor force with appropriate skills and must be able to mobilize that labor force in a flexible and efficient way.

Over the past several decades, the proportion of small businesses has declined with the growth of large national and multinational corporations. Nevertheless, there are industries and industry segments where small businesses are viable.[11] This is clearly a necessary condition for ethnic entrepreneurship; it is in those segments that immigrant businesses are found.[12] Moreover, groups of immigrants from the same country and background will concentrate in small business only under certain conditions. For example, comparing two groups of Chinese who immigrated to Jamaica and to Guyana from the same region, Orlando Patterson found that only the group that settled in Jamaica was concentrated in small business. A different situation in Guyana resulted in a different outcome.[13]

Given appropriate conditions, explanation of immigrant concentration in self-employment should indicate why the foreign born have advantageous access to the other requirements for successful entrepreneurship. Although research on immigrant business does not approach the issue in this way, most studies at least implicitly work from a set of requirements for the success of small businesses and argue that immigrants indeed meet those requirements more than natives.

One argument suggests that cultural factors predispose some ethnic groups to entrepreneurship.[14] This explanation therefore focuses on the second factor listed above: entrepreneurial orientation.

Another much more comprehensive strand of research focuses on solidaristic behavior among members of ethnic groups as a fundamental explanation for immigrant self-employment. This solidarity is based either on culturally based familial or ethnic networks imported directly from the sending country or on a defensive reaction to host country hostility.[15]   Although not disagreeing with the cultural predisposition explanation, this argument suggests that solidarity is a resource that raises capital, establishes networks among businessmen and suppliers, and provides access to the cheap labor of more recently arrived countrymen.   Some studies have suggested that ethnic solidarity is used to control entry into industries and regulate particular markets, thereby creating monopoly-like conditions that provide a protected environment for immigrant business.[16] Indeed, Wilson and Portes offer this argument as an explanation of why immigrant businesses apparently provide employment conditions superior to those offered in native-owned secondary-sector firms.[17]

The argument in this chapter and the last suggest that there are additional explanations for some of these factors and that some important causes of immigrant self-employment are neglected. First, although cultural predisposition may indeed explain variations in the incidence of self-employment among different immigrant groups, the overrepresentation in small business of immigrants from almost all ethnic and cultural backgrounds suggests that the cultural milieu that shapes the employment of the native born in the United States is in some sense antientrepreneurial. In any case, an explanation for the concentration of the foreign born in self-employment can be found in the characteristics of the immigration process itself.

The initial motivations of immigrants are often frankly entrepreneurial. Although their goals at first may be directed toward the sending country, as immigrants develop attachments to the host society, it is hardly surprising that their entrepreneurial aspirations are reoriented along with those attachments. Even when immigrants do not aspire to self-employment, to the extent that they view their stay as temporary or transitional and conceive of it in terms of investment, their savings rates will be higher and workweeks longer. These in turn enhance eventual entrepreneurial options.

Moreover, the experience that many immigrants have in the informal sector of the sending countries also increases their orientation toward entrepreneurship. To be sure, all informal sector workers are not self-employed; nevertheless, the sector does constitute an environment in which petty entrepreneurship is the central dynamic for income generation and, in many cases, economic mobilty.

And because many unskilled jobs that are open to newly arrived immigrants are in small businesses, their early experiences in the receiving economy also increase their exposure to entrepreneurial activities. Then the gradual process of adjustment creates incentives for immigrants to seek economic mobility in those industries where entrepreneurship constitutes one of the major opportunities.

Indeed, in the extensive research on immigrant entrepreneurship, the internal labor process of immigrant firms has received little attention. This process not only mobilizes cheap labor, a phenomenon that much research does emphasize, but it also provides flexibility and at the same time trains the future cadre of skilled workers and entrepreneurs. The labor process also reduces the need for capital and thereby eases the search for financing.

Familial relationships and broader ethnic networks also play an important role in recruiting labor; in setting an environment favorable to training within the firm; in establishing business relationships with suppliers, customers, and the competition; and in raising capital. However, although these relationships certainly have cultural and ethnic roots, the immigration process itself also selects immigrants who are integrated into networks.

Moreover, judging from the restaurant industry, the networks and relationships are less formal and organized than some authors suggest. No formal credit associations were used by the restaurateurs interviewed for this study and no evidence of price or entry regulation, vertical integration, or other joint monopolistic activities were found. Moreover, the fierce ethnic competition among Hispanic garment firms and Korean vegetable stands hardly suggests successful market control.[18]

In the end, the existence of immigrant-type restaurants and similar establishments depends on the arrival of new immigrants. When a particular immigrant stream abates or stops, owners must turn to other ethnic groups. Although immigrant owners who worked themselves up through the industry often absorb immigrants from other countries into the traditional labor process, the viability of the process weakens as the relationships become more distant. In the extreme, ethnicity, instead of strengthening production and skills training processes, may become a barrier to the effective operation of those processes. After all, ethnic antagonism is the complementary side of ethnic solidarity. Therefore, when the owner and the workers are from different ethnic groups, the long and arbitrary hours and the low wages appear more exploitative and unfair. At this point, some firms can try to reduce the need for skills; other firms can move into higher-priced markets, upgrade their employment, and establish more formalized procedures and training methods; and still other firms, for which none of these strategies works, simply disappear. Thus, in response to immigration restrictions, the ethnic restaurant will not necessarily disappear;

rather, the distinctive labor process now used in many of those restaurants will weaken, and the techniques and labor force of restaurants serving ethnic foods will more closely resemble those in native-owned restaurants.

The current concentration of immigrants in self-employment emerges from the existing social and economic context. The available production technologies, the structure of the economy as well as the status associated with employment in particular occupations and industries all influence the extent to which immigrants and natives are drawn to and succeed in self-employment.

The analysis presented points to the dynamic character of the immigration process as a fundamental cause of the immigrant propensity for self-employment. The move between two economies and the reduced value of skills learned in the sending country; the lingering identification with two societies and cultures; the investment perspective inherent in immigration; the pattern of gradual adaptation to the new setting; and the continued use of the social networks that brought the immigrants in the first place all enhance the chances that newcomers will gravitate toward self-employment. This is not to deny the contribution of cultural factors and solidaristic behavior but rather to state that they cannot be viewed in static terms. Petty ethnic entrepreneurship is a transitional phenomenon rooted in the change itself.

The Garment Industry

The garment industry illustrates important aspects of the immigrant labor market role as it is analyzed in this book.[19] Perhaps the most obvious aspect of the role of immigrants is their availability as very low-wage workers. But immigrants also provide a supply of skilled and entrepreneurial labor in industries or industrial sectors where labor markets and skill-acquisition processes are informal, uncertain, and unorganized. And for the same reasons, immigrants, more than other groups, are able to use these industries for economic mobility.

As with the restaurant industry, the immigrant role in the garment industry can be more easily understood by analyzing the labor process in different segments of the garment industry. In his study of the industry, Roger Waldinger emphasizes two types of production—standardized and unstandardized. Over the past twenty-five years, standardization and accompanying automation and mass production have come to dominate the manufacture of many clothing lines including underwear, blue jeans, and men's shirts. Waldinger argues that the growth of demand has led to standardization of the production of higher-priced garments as well.[20] The production of standardized goods is most efficiently carried out in large plants with a low-paid, low-skilled labor force. Because demand is predictable, flexibility in production or proximity to design and marketing centers such as New York City carry little weight in locational decision-making or production planning. Given the relatively high wages in New York's garment industry, employment in the production of standardized goods in New York steadily diminished when the post–World War II boom began to justify substantial new investments in lower-wage regions and abroad. Those firms that have continued to produce in New York do so for special reasons. Thus Waldinger argues that "The age and experience of the owners go far in accounting for continued persistence. Most have succeeded in finding a market niche where head-to-head competition with lower labor-cost firms can be minimized. Extensive information networks and long-standing connections with buyers and suppliers help contain direct competition with large out-of-town producers of standardized goods."[21] More recently, the significant shrinkage of the wage differential between New York and other regions and the associated availability of low-cost immigrant labor are undoubtedly factors that have helped these firms survive.

The bulk of garment employment remaining in New York is therefore concentrated in the production of nonstandardized goods. Waldinger argues that a large part of these products consist of low-priced but styled garments particularly for women. The styling of these low-priced goods is subject to rapidly changing and uncertain demand and because of this uncertainty and the need for fast turnaround, location near New York's marketing and design centers is much more important. New York also retained some employment engaged in supplementary production of more standardized goods, for example, when demand for a particular item has been underestimated. When this happens, additional production is needed quickly and demand cannot be met by importing; thus again proximity and flexibility are crucial. But Waldinger points out that this demand for New York production, especially for low-priced styled garments, is still price elastic. The moderate- and low-income consumers who buy these goods are likely to purchase the less-varied garments that can be mass-produced and imported if the prices for stylish locally produced items rise too sharply.

The structure and organization of production in the garment industry of New York have evolved in such a way as to accommodate the need for a flexibile capacity to produce nonstandardized goods at low cost on short notice. A central component of that structure is the contracting system. The contracting system separates design and marketing, which are done by the manufacturers, from production—sewing and cutting—which is done by the contractor. In this system, most of the contractors are immigrant owners, employing almost exclusively immigrant workers. This division of labor offers advantages to both manufacturers and immigrant contractors. Manufacturers can respond quickly to changing demands without maintaining and training a large labor force, part of which would be idle when demand slackens.

The contracting system also offers several advantages to marginal immigrant owners. Since variable demand reduces the usefulness of advanced production techniques, contractors can operate successfully with used, hand-guided machines that can be installed in almost any space. Thus capital and occupancy costs are low. And although pressured production of varied shorter runs does require some skills, they are the types of skills that can be learned easily on the job. Moreover, as Waldinger states: "The division of labor between manufacturer and contractor spares the contractor the costs of raw materials as well as the risks of accumulating inventories. More importantly, this arrangement reduces the contractor's role to the tasks of recruiting and organizing labor functions which the immigrant contractor, with direct connections to the labor force, is ideally suited to perform."[22] These opportunities channel immigrant-owned firms into contracting work. Thus of the ninety-six immigrant firms that Waldinger studied, ninety-one were engaged in contracting for manufacturers.[23]

The picture of the labor process in the immigrant garment firm presented by Waldinger is similar to what we have seen in small restaurants. The family is the most important source of labor as well as capital, and when the labor needs are too great for the immediate family members, employers rely almost exclusively on kinship and community networks. As is the case in restaurants, this network hiring provides information about the new recruits and strengthens their attachment to the firm. It also facilitates training by reducing the risks that an employer's training efforts are wasted. As one owner interviewed by Waldinger stated: "I won't provide training to unknown workers who come in looking for a job. When I need somebody, I ask the workers to bring in a relative. That way one worker helps another; and I don't have to worry about training someone who will later go find work in another shop."[24] These arrangements also promote immigration and provide employers with easy access to cheap labor. Finally, informal links facilitate adjustments to rapidly changing labor force needs—a crucial factor in the functioning of the industry niche that has slowed the decline of garment employment in New York.

The garment industry provides another illustration of the relationship between low-paid immigrant labor, marginal immigrant entrepreneurship, and the informal relationships and networks that bind these together. Indeed, as Waldinger found, most of the owners worked for other immigrants before working for themselves. Clearly the low-skill level of many recent immigrants is not the only factor that defines the role of the immigrant in this industry. If it were, then a common ethnicity between workers and owners would not be such a central feature of garment production. Even when native-born garment industry employers use recent Hispanic immigrants as low-wage labor, these owners are likely to be descendants of Jewish or Italian immigrants who learned their production and managerial skills when members of those ethnic groups dominated the ranks of both workers and owners in the industry. But if established owners can shift to a new source of labor, it is almost unheard of for an entrepreneur to enter the labor-intensive, nonstandardized segments of the industry without close ties to the industry's labor force.

In both the garment and the restaurant industry, immigrants play a dual role in the labor market. On the one hand, they provide a supply of labor for extremely low-quality jobs. But on the other hand, immigrants provide a labor supply for skilled jobs and entrepreneurial positions that are characterized by uncertain and disorganized processes of skill acquisition. Moreover, the two poles of this dual role are closely linked. They reflect the conditions under which these workers undertake their initial migration and the interaction of the characteristics of their early jobs with the changing goals and orientation that they experience during the settlement process.

Notes

1. Illsoo Kim, *New Urban Immigrants: The Korean Community in New York* (Princeton, N.J.: Princeton University Press, 1981); and Joan Greenwald, "Niches in a New Land," *Time*, July 8, 1985, p. 73.

2. Marcia Freedman, "Urban Labor Markets and Ethnicity: Segments and Shelters Re-examined," in Lionel Maldonado and Joan Moore, eds., *Urban Ethnicity in the United States: New and Old Minorities* (Beverly Hills, Cal.: Sage Publications, 1985).

3. Roger Waldinger, *Through the Eye of the Needle: Immigrant Enterprise in New York's Garment Trades* (New York, N.Y.: New York University Press, 1986); Diana Balmori, "Hispanic Immigrants in the Construction Industry: New York City, 1960–1982," Occasional Paper No. 38 (New York, N.Y.: New York University, Center for Latin American and Caribbean Studies, May 1983);

and Carmenza Gallo, "The Construction Industry in New York City: Immigrant and Black Entrepreneurs," Working Paper (New York, N.Y.: Columbia University, Conservation of Human Resources, 1983).

4. One hundred and fifty-six restaurants were surveyed in the three boroughs of Manhattan, Queens, and Brooklyn. Ninety-two were owned by first-generation immigrants who were not from Northwestern Europe. Sixty of the ninety-two were owned by Greeks, Italians, and Chinese. Of the remaining sixty-four, nine were owned by immigrants from Western Europe.

5. U.S. Bureau of the Census, *Census of Population: 1970, Public Use Samples of Basic Records (5 percent Sample), New York* (Washington, D.C.: GPO); and U.S. Bureau of the Census, *Census of Population and Housing: 1980, Public Use Microdata Samples (A Sample), New York* (Washington, D.C.: GPO).

6. Kenneth L. Wilson and Alejandro Portes, "Immigrant Enclaves: An Analysis of the Labor Market Experiences of Cubans in Miami," *American Journal of Sociology* 86 (September 1980): 295–319.

7. Wilson and Portes, 1980, p. 315.

8. Harry Herman, "Dishwashers and Proprietors: Macedonians in Toronto's Restaurant Trade," in Sandra Wallman, ed., *Ethnicity at Work* (London: Macmillan, 1979), p. 70.

9. Industrial financial data indicate that the annual sales/capital ratio in restaurants is approximately 3.6. See Daryl D. Wyckoff and Earl Sasser, *The Chain-Restaurant Industry* (Lexington, Mass.: Lexington Books, 1978), p. xlviii. In 1982, restaurants with five or six employees had average annual sales of $136,000. See U.S. Bureau of the Census, *Census of Retail Trade: 1982, Industry Series, Establishment and Firm Size, RC 82-I-1* (Washington, D.C.: GPO), table 2. Capital costs for these establishments were therefore approximately $38,000. Using sales figures for establishments with payrolls but with no paid employees *at the time of the survey* for a similar calculation yields capital costs for family-operated units.

10. There were 10,000 eating and drinking places in New York in 1980. If the sample drawn from the telephone book is representative, at least one-half of them were owned by immigrants. Furthermore, a comparison between telephone lists and lists provided by the New York State Department of Labor revealed that many immigrant restaurants, especially small establishments in immigrant neighborhoods, had no phones. Therefore the results of the telephone survey understated the number of immigrant restaurants. It is safe to say there there were at least 6,000 immigrant-owned restaurants in the city, and because many were owned by more than one person, the number of immigrant owners was considerably higher, perhaps 10,000. Because the restaurants in this sector were small, the ratio of employees to owners was low, no more than 5 to 1 (57 percent of all restaurants in New York in 1978 employed fewer than 5 people) and probably less. The ratio of all immigrant restaurant workers to immigrant owners was higher, certainly no more than 10 to 1. If there were about 10,000 owners and if *all* of the approximately 100,000 workers in the industry were immigrants, then the ratio would be 10 to 1. Of

course there were illegal residents and other immigrants who do not appear in the statistics, but there were also many native born who do.

11. Suzanne Berger and Michael Piore, *Dualism and Discontinuity in Industrial Societies* (New York, N.Y.: Cambridge University Press, 1980.)

12. Waldinger, 1986, chapter 2.

13. Orlando Patterson concluded that in "the case of Jamaica, economic conditions were such that the best interests of the group were served by an exclusive concern with retail trade, *and that success in this venture allowed for,* and *reinforced, a choice of ethnic consolidation based on cultural distinctiveness. . . .*

On the other hand, we have seen how, in the Guyanese context, economic and social conditions were such that a wider range of occupational choices was in the best interests of the Chinese, and how, in pursuing these occupations, the choice of synthetic creolization and the abandonment of Chinese culture were the most rational courses of action."

Orlando Patterson, "Context and Choice in Ethnic Allegiance: A Theoretical Framework and Caribbean Case Study," in Nathan Glazer, ed., *Ethnicity* (Cambridge, Mass.: Harvard University Press, 1975) p. 347.

14. Cultural arguments are difficult to specify. Indeed this argument is as much a popular conception as a research hypothesis. For a critique, see Waldinger, 1986, chapter 1.

15. Ivan H. Light, *Ethnic Enterprise in America: Business and Welfare Among Chinese, Japanese, and Blacks* (Berkeley, Cal.: University of California Press, 1972); and Edna Bonacich and John Modell, *The Economic Basis of Ethnic Solidarity* (Berkeley, Cal.: University of California Press, 1980).

16. Light, 1972; and John Modell, *The Economics and Politics of Racial Accommodation* (Urbana, Ill.: University of Illinois Press, 1977).

17. Wilson and Portes, 1980.

18. Waldinger, 1986, chapter 2.

19. This section is based on Waldinger's recent case studies of the garment industry in New York City, "Immigration and Industrial Change: A Case Study of Immigrants in the New York City Garment Industry" (PhD dissertation, Department of Sociology, Harvard University, 1983); and Waldinger, 1986.

20. Waldinger, 1983, chapter 3.

21. Waldinger, 1983, p. 157.

22. Waldinger, 1983, p. 63.

23. Waldinger, 1983, p. 93.

24. Waldinger, 1983, p. 67.

4

Weak Labor Force
Attachment and
Low-Skilled Natives

Many of the country's lowest-skilled and lowest-paying jobs are held by young workers and by adult women with low levels of educational attainment. Many youth and women have also experienced serious problems in finding work. Unemployment rates for all teenagers have consistently been above 20 percent; unemployment for minority youth tops 50 percent in many cities. The economic position of female-headed families has also become an increasingly urgent national policy issue.

Despite the potential impact of immigration restriction on the employment of youth and adult women, our knowledge of the interaction between these groups and immigrants barely extends beyond the observation that members of all three groups tend to have low-skilled jobs. Listing several important differences among the groups that might differentiate their labor market roles is easy; yet little attention has been paid to the implications of these differences or to empirical measurement of the impact of immigration on youth and female employment.

This chapter compares the labor market roles of teenagers, women, and immigrants in the restaurant industry. In particular, it focuses on the labor process in the fast-food sector, which depends primarily on teenagers, and in the intermediate sector, which relies on women. The chapter ends with an additional example from the supermarket industry.

The Fast-Food Sector

The fast-food sector represents the forefront of the main technological and personnel trends in the restaurant industry. Although previously the typical restaurant was staffed at all levels by adult men and women with relatively low levels of educational attainment, today almost 50 percent of the restaurant market is served by fast-food outlets that employ a large number of short-tenure teenagers and are managed by college graduates with some formal management training.

In a 1981 survey conducted for this study of fast-food chains in Manhattan, 65 percent of the nonmanagerial employees were under twenty-one years of age. National data indicate that in 1983, 70 percent of all fast-food workers were sixteen to twenty years old, and 85 percent, twenty-four years or younger.[1] Females accounted for 66 percent of the total work force and about 63 percent of the teenage work force in the sector.[2]

In contrast to the sector's dependence on youth, representatives of Burger King, McDonald's, Wendy's, and Nedick's all reported that they employed few immigrants in fast-food outlets in New York City. No national data are available on foreign-born employment in the sector, but Hispanics accounted for 5 percent of the fast-food work force while according to the 1980 census, 6 percent of the population was Hispanic.[3] Of all Hispanics in the United States, about one-quarter were foreign born.[4]

Fast-food establishments have built their success on low prices, fast service, and advertising. The cost savings derive from a limited menu that allows almost complete standardization, high-volume purchasing, the use of expensive and highly specialized machinery, off-premises food preparation, and simplified work procedures. This production process has obviated the need for skills associated with preparing or serving food and, along with the use of disposable plates and utensils, has reduced the labor share of fast-food sales to about 20 percent. Some fast-food managers interviewed for this study reported labor shares as low as 12 percent. In comparison, the average labor share for all eating places is 28 percent, whereas it is close to 50 percent for full-service restaurants if tips are included.[5]

Over the past twenty years, the growth of the fast-food sector has been responsible for much of the growth of the restaurant industry. Fast-food restaurants correspond roughly to eating places referred to in the *The Census of Retail Trade* as "refreshment places." Between 1967 and 1982, real sales in refreshment places grew 177 percent, compared to total restaurant real growth of 46 percent.[6] Table 4.1 shows the

TABLE 4.1
Share of Refreshment-Place Sales in Sales of Eating Places,
United States and New York SMSA, Selected Years, 1958–1982
(in percentages)

Year	United States	New York SMSA
1958	3.8	n.a.
1963	14.6	10.0
1967	19.0	13.2
1972	29.1	17.8
1977	36.9	26.0
1982	38.5	a

aThe definition of the New York SMSA changed in 1980.

Source: U.S. Bureau of the Census, *Census of Business, 1958, 1962,* and *1967, Retail Trade Area Statistics, United States and New York* (Washington, D.C.: GPO); and U.S. Bureau of the Census, *Census of Retail Trade, 1972, 1977,* and *1982, Geographic Area Series, United States and New York* (Washington, D.C.: GPO).

refreshment-place market share in the United States and in the New York Standard Metropolitan Statistical Area (SMSA) between 1958 and 1982.

The fast-food sector represents the extreme of the trend in the industry in which production is shifted to line operations in the manufacturing sector. The role of the fast-food outlet is limited to a retail function. This is particularly significant from the point of view of the possible impact of changes in the level of immigration because it increases the vulnerability of the industry's employment to interregional or even international competition. For example, local dishwashing services can be replaced by imported paper and plastic products; instead of locally laundered linens, disposable products are used; and the use of pre-prepared, precut hamburgers and french fries, ready-made desserts, and so forth, all potentially reduce the local component of restaurant employment.

The growth of the fast-food sector and of its distinctive production processes has encouraged and in turn has been reinforced by the growth of chains. Two Harvard Business School professors stated in 1978: "There has been unprecedented growth during the past two decades in chain restaurants, arising from the introduction of new approaches to management, control, purchasing, technology, facilities, and financing that have brought a latter-day industrial revolution to a previously fragmented industry."[7]

In 1967, sales by chain units were 24 percent of total fast-food sales, with sales by chains with more than 100 units accounting for 3 percent. By 1972, the total share of chains had grown to 41 percent with most of the growth occurring among the largest chains. In those five years, the share for chains with more than 100 units grew from 3 percent to 15 percent.[8] By 1978, chains probably accounted for more than 75 percent of fast-food sales.[9]

The growth of chains has influenced the job structure of the fast-food sector. Chains promote the use of a technology that requires few skills, and with the possible exception of "approaches to management," none of the developments that spurred the growth of chains cited above relate to the training of skilled labor.

Fast-food workers perform a variety of tasks including cleaning, cooking, food preparation, and taking orders and money. According to a 1983 survey of fast-food outlets, hourly workers tended to be assigned primarily to one task although they usually had some experience working in several.[10] Although employees were sometimes engaged in ordering or inventory control, the large majority of the tasks in fast-food restaurants were low paid, required minimal skills, and could be learned in a few hours or days. Average hourly rates in 1983 were about $3.70.[11]

Apparently, some hourly employees do take on lower-level supervision and training roles.[12] Nevertheless, few have the opportunity to move up to the salaried positions of assistant manager and manager. Most fast-food companies have an informal policy of not recruiting management trainees from their lower-level work force.[13]

Fast-food production minimizes the costs of employee turnover. The elimination of cooking skills reduces the problems associated with training and retaining a labor force.[14] Because workers are rotated, each can perform several tasks so fill-ins can be found easily on short notice among other employees. In large chains, as long as the instability is anticipated, hiring can be adjusted. Some chains simply hire a given number of workers each week regardless of the actual number of openings.

Not only can fast-food establishments operate successfully with high turnover, but part-time, short-term employment is actually advantageous because the industry has significant seasonal and daily fluctuations. As long as there is constant turnover, seasonal fluctuations can be absorbed by slowing or accelerating hiring. Most food arrives at the outlet already prepared except for final heating or frying, which must be done close to the time when the food is served. The size of the work force must therefore respond directly to the fluctuations of business over the day. Part-timers provide this flexibility.

Finally, a stable work force would be a more likely target for unionization. Therefore, an unattached and uncommitted work force is fundamental to antiunion strategy that at least in the fast-food segment has been successful. Even when fast-food chains or outlets are unionized, the union seems to make little difference. As one regional personnel manager said, "We have sweetheart contracts with several locals. They are reasonably undemanding in negotiations." Unionized fast-food workers in one chain in New York earned no more than ten or fifteen cents above the minimum wage.

Attracting full-time, full-year workers would require paying enough to support an individual or a family. As one manager said, "Almost all of our jobs are part-time and are not suited to workers who support a family."

As a result, the majority of the employees in the sector are part-time, short-term workers. A turnover rate of 300 percent is common in some chains.[15] One district manager of a chain reported a turnover rate as high as 500 percent in some restaurants. Most reported a turnover of about 100 percent. To be sure, high annual turnover figures can exaggerate instability. For example, a few positions may turn over frequently while most workers at any given time have longer tenure. Ivan Charner and Bryna Shore Fraser found that about 53 percent of their national sample had at least twelve months of tenure.[16]

The results of a telephone survey, displayed in Table 4.2, of twenty-five fast-food outlets selected at random from a list of the Manhattan units of four large chains, suggest that in New York City this instability may be greater than in the country as a whole. Sixty

TABLE 4.2
Employee Characteristics in Sample of Chain Restaurant Outlets in Manhattan, New York, 1981

	Number of		Percent		
Chain	Outlets Surveyed	Nonmanagerial Employees	Part-time	Under 21 Years Old	Employed Less Than One Year
1	6	233	61	80	61
2	8	324	79	62	73
3	4	48	71	71	58
4	7	96	41	39	40

Source: Data collected by the author.

percent of the workers in Chains 1, 2, and 3 were part-timers with less than one year's tenure. Chain 4, which had the most stable work force, had experienced a significant relative decline in its business the previous ten years. In contrast, Chain 2 has been successful in New York despite its high employee turnover.

Management jobs also have been simplified. The large chains establish highly routinized procedures for these employees. For example, McDonald's distributes calendars to its managers to remind them of such things as when to contract for snow removal. Therefore, high levels of management turnover are also an accepted part of fast-food operations. According to one industry analyst, turnover among managers, even in successful chains, is about 25 percent a year.[17] The personnel manager of a large and growing chain in New York said that annual turnover among assistant managers was 50 percent. For another successful chain, turnover in this group was 75 percent a year.

Nevertheless, fast-food economics depends on low-paid assistant managers who are willing to take on extra responsibility with only a small increase in pay. For example, at the time of the interviews for this study, one chain paid starting managers $180 a week while another paid managers of stores employing forty to sixty people $280 a week. Only the managers of large and growing outlets, managers of serveral stores, or franchise holders themselves make as much as the median individual annual income.

In fact, adjusting for hours worked, assistant managers often earn lower wages than crew members. Managers emphasized that assistant managers, despite their low pay, were central to the success of the operation because they were responsible for motivating the crews and preventing theft. Presumably, assistant managers take on these responsibilities because of the possibilities of future promotion beyond the store level into corporate regional or national management, or in some cases, to high-volume stores. For this motivational structure to work, however, the chain must be growing. Chains that stop opening new outlets have fewer opportunities to promote young managers and begin to have more serious problems in recruiting and retaining assistant managers. In chains that have stopped growing, assistant manager jobs are carried out less effectively and store-level business and profits usually decline.[18] This contrasts with the motivational structure in the immigrant-owned sectors where immigrants anticipate opportunities for skilled work or entrepreneurship within the industry rather than within one firm or chain.

Judging from the current low level of employment of immigrants in this sector, a decline in immigration would have little effect on the fast-food sector. Indeed, although real wages for dishwashers and cooks have been falling for a decade, the real wages of fast-food counter workers actually grew during the early 1980s.[19] To be sure, this was also a period when the fast-food sector was growing, a factor that could have created demand-side pressure for increased wages. Nevertheless, the industry sectors where wages fell were also growing. Thus it can at least be said that the increasing supply of immigrants could not be sufficiently tapped by owners in the fast-food sector to keep wages down.

The aging of the baby boom cohort may in the future draw more immigrants into the fast-food labor force. Although to some extent the shortage of teenagers may be alleviated, at least in large cities, as the demand for their labor in industries outside of the retail sector declines.[20] In any case, fast-food outlets can still draw on housewives for part-time work, and there appears to be a trend toward the use of older workers and recent retirees.

If anything, the sector might grow as a result of immigration restriction, given that it would no longer have to compete with immigrant-owned restaurants. Thus, if Greek-owned coffee shops, Italian pizzerias, or Chinese take-out restaurants were not available, some of the demand could be served by McDonald's, Shoney's, Wendy's, or similar establishments. In this way, immigration restriction would have the effect of reducing overall skill levels in the industry rather than increasing them as the simple models predict. Data from 1970 do indicate that the relative size of the immigrant population in an SMSA was negatively associated with the fast-food share of the total restaurant market. Although this relationship is statistically significant, it is not large: The estimate suggests that a 10 percent decline in the immigrant share of the population would increase the fast-food share only 1 percent.[21] Indeed, the overall growth of the fast-food sector has overwhelmed this small competitive effect and the employment of both teenagers and immigrants has grown over the past decade.

The Intermediate Sector

The intermediate sector accounts for about 40 percent of restaurant sales in the United States but only about 15 percent in New York. Restaurants in this sector are characterized by price, skill, and employment-stability levels that lie between the fast-food and the full-service sectors. Typical intermediate restaurants include coffee shops and steak houses.

Two characteristics distinguish this intermediate-restaurant sector from the others. First, unlike the fast-food sector, intermediate-sector restaurants have table or counter service, although service is less formal than in the full-service sector. Second, although the menu is more extensive than in the fast-food sector, it usually consists of a limited number of easily prepared items. The limited menus, the extensive use of pre-prepared foods, and the informal atmosphere obviate the need for the well-developed cooking and serving skills that predominate in the full-service sector.

Employment trends in intermediate sector restaurants are also consistent with the general developments in skill levels, food preparation techniques, and management procedures in the restaurant industry, although to a lesser degree than in the fast-food sector. Nevertheless, the production process in the intermediate sector is not so resistant to the problems of instability as is that of the fast-food sector. This difference is reflected by comparing the labor forces in the two sectors. Whereas the fast-food sector depends on teenagers, adult women form the core of the intermediate-sector work force.

In the United States in 1980, 60 percent of the industry's employed labor force was female.[22] Although females account for 66 percent of fast-food employment, they tend to be young. Moreover, women are probably underrepresented in the full-service sector. Therefore, the overall figure of 60 percent for the industry as a whole understates the importance of adult women in the intermediate sector.

The contrast between the male and female roles in the industry emerges in the sex distribution of the age cohorts of restaurant workers. The overrepresentation of women increases in the older cohorts. In 1980, 45 percent of the employed sixteen- to nineteen-year-olds in the industry were male. Only 38 percent of the twenty-five and older group were males. Males twenty-five and over accounted for only about 19 percent of the work force.[23]

In New York City, immigrants are also employed in this sector. Indeed, almost all of the unskilled kitchen jobs in the sector and many of the more skilled cooking jobs are held by foreign-born men. Some older adult native-born black men were found in the skilled cooking jobs, although few blacks held intermediate sector dishwashing jobs.

In New York's lower-priced intermediate-sector restaurants, such as coffee shops, black and white women in their late twenties and older dominate the waitress and cashier positions. But the dining room and lower-level managerial jobs in the more expensive intermediate-sector restaurants, such as steak houses, are dominated by men and women in their early and midtwenties. These workers are drawn from the large supply of unemployed and underemployed actors, actresses, dancers, and other artists who work in restaurants between jobs or part-time to support themselves while they pursue their careers. This labor supply also plays an important role in the full-service sector.

Chains are also important in this sector. In the late 1970s, whereas 80 percent of the food-service market was held by the intermediate and fast-food restaurants, between 35 and 40 percent was held by chains with sales of $15 million or more. Because the top seven hamburger chains represented 12 percent of the entire market, it is reasonable to assume that over half of chain sales were in the fast-food sector.[24]   Therefore, nationally, somewhat less than half of the intermediate-sector sales could be attributed to these large chains. Certainly this percentage would be considerably larger if the cutoff point were below $15 million. The chains in this sector tend to be smaller than those in the fast-food sector. In New York, although the intermediate sector is smaller than it is nationally, chains seem to be particularly important, especially at the lower end of the price range. As the telephone survey indicated, there are few native-owned, independent, moderately priced restaurants. Over the last five years, the importance of chains in this sector has undoubtedly grown.

There is considerable diversity in the technology that is used in the sector. On the one hand, intermediate restaurants do not use a production process that depends on machines to complete the final heating and assembly of food that is already prepared. On the other hand, menus are usually so simple that the food requires no complicated preparation. Pre-prepared foods are used extensively, but the larger menus prevent the extreme standardization that characterizes the fast-food sector.

Due to the low level of required skills, the job structure is truncated in this sector. Most nonmanagerial restaurant workers have one of three jobs: cook, waiter/waitress, or dishwasher/porter. Although dishwashers' wages are still close to the minimum wage, the cooking skills are more demanding than those required in the fast-food sector; therefore, there are more opportunities for upward occupational and earnings mobility in the kitchen. In New York in 1981, intermediate-sector cooks started at $4.00 to $5.00 an hour and earned more after several years. One broilerman, having worked in an inexpensive New York steak house for eighteen years, earned $8.00 an hour. Nevertheless, the skills required in both the dining room and the kitchen are less advanced than those in the full-service sector. For the most part, cooks in this sector are most accurately classified as semiskilled. They must learn to prepare a small number of relatively simple dishes, often using ingredients that are already semiprepared (pancake mixes, canned soups, precut steaks, etc.). Even the most skilled acquire their training informally on the job. Formal cooking training is rare in the sector. Indeed, organized on-the-job training is generally limited to explaining the particular procedures of the restaurant. Managers speak of devoting no more than a few hours to training new employees.[25]

In the chains in the sector, there are mobility opportunities in store-level management and eventually within the corporate hierarchy. Nevertheless, as in the fast-food sector, the chains tend to hire their management trainees from among outside applicants with levels of educational attainment higher than those of the hourly employees.

Employment stability in this sector falls between the revolving door turnover of the fast-food sector and the more stable employment of the full-service sector. Of the ten respondents from this sector in New York that had been in business for five or more years, seven reported that several workers had been in their employ for more than five years. In another establishment that had been in business for about four years, five of the nine workers had been employed since the restaurant's establishment. One manager said that more than 25 percent of his workers had been with him for more than ten years. Of the five in business for fifteen years, four had at least one worker who had been there for fifteen years or more.

Nevertheless, many restaurant managers in this sector complain about instability, but they realize, as do their fast-food colleagues, that over the long term, "full-time stable workers want full-time stable pay," as one manager put it. In order to pay the relatively low wages that prevail in the sector, managers accept workers whose employment fits into their other activities. Although the limited menu and rudimentary skills in the intermediate sector obviate the need for fully attached workers, its production process requires more stability than the fast-food sector. Because the jobs tend to be more differentiated than in fast-food outlets, the workers are not so easily interchanged. It is therefore harder to replace people who do not show up.

At this point, it is useful to ask why paternalism, which is so important in the management of unskilled workers in the full-service sector, plays a much smaller role in the management of workers in the fast-food and intermediate sectors. One explanation concerns the size of the firms in the various sectors. The intermediate and fast-food sectors are dominated by chains. Thus the owners may never see the workers, much less get to know them well.[26] Moreover, the managers, who might be in a position to develop closer ties to the workers, themselves have relatively high levels of turnover. Contrasting production processes is another source of differentiation. Although many workers in all three sectors need few general skills, firm-specific experience is more important in the full-service sector; therefore, owners of these restaurants have a greater incentive to keep turnover low. Heavy reliance on part-timers also thwarts the development of personal relationships in fast-food and intermediate restaurants.

Judging from the situation in New York, intermediate-sector establishments located in cities with large immigrant populations would have to find a new source of workers for their unskilled kitchen jobs and for some of their skilled workers if immigration were restricted. Nationally, women form the core of the sector's labor force, and it would seem likely that the industry would turn to this group in the event of a reduction in immigration. College students and other young adults could also be tapped for these jobs. But the use of these groups would set up additional incentives to standardize food-preparation techniques and to rely more on pre-prepared food.

It is also likely that this sector would grow as a result of immigration restriction. As we have seen, it is relatively much smaller in New York, where so many immigrants are available, than in the nation. Immigrant restaurants also appear to compete most directly with intermediate establishments. Furthermore, interviews with managers in the full-service sector suggest that they, too, could adopt techniques similar to those that predominate in the intermediate sector if they had trouble finding immigrant workers.

The Retail Food Industry

The segmentation within the retail food industry is in many ways similar to the segmentation in restaurants.[27] At one extreme, there is a modern sector that combines modern management techniques and advanced technology with a primarily unskilled, high-turnover labor force. At the other extreme lies a sector of small businesses that rely on more traditional business practices and a longer-term, more stable, although still low-paid labor force. As is the case in the immigrant restaurant sector, the small-firm sector in the retail food industry relies primarily on informal relationships and networks for recruiting, training, and indeed for many aspects of the operation of the firm. Finally, the chains of small "convenience" stores have some similarity to the intermediate sectors of the restaurant industry.

In New York City in 1980, the retail food industry employed approximately 15,100 sixteen- to nineteen-year-olds and accounted for almost 14 percent of all youth jobs in the city. In 1980, 32 percent of the industry's employment in New York City was foreign born, and about twenty-three out of every 100 employees were under twenty years of age. No other industry was more dependent on youth. And the youth themselves were no less dependent on the industry for employment.[28]

Teenagers in the industry are primarily employed as cashiers and stock clerks in supermarkets, jobs requiring few skills. Indeed although managers reported that a fifth-grade math proficiency was generally expected, the introduction of computerized cash registers has weakened even that requirement. As one manager pointed out: "With changes in technology, the importance of arithmetic has diminished."

The jobs held by teenagers in this industry require limited training. The training period, during which the newly hired person works under the supervision of a more experienced worker, lasts two to five days; typically, this is followed by a second week during which the new worker is stationed alongside more experienced employees. By the third week, the new worker is expected to be functioning without assistance. Teenagers usually start as cashiers, and there are only limited opportunities for mobility. There is some branching out into other jobs, mainly various clerking positions in grocery and produce departments, but there is little further advancement after these initial placements. Most of the personnel managers, to be sure, knew of individual teenagers who had moved from part-time employment into the permanent job hierarchy, but these were seen as exceptions. Teenagers are almost all employed as part-timers: Roughly 90 percent of the supermarkets' part-time labor force consists of young people aged sixteen to nineteen. Moreover, the demand for part-time workers is intense and constant:

> I am always short of labor. I've never had a moment in this job when I've needed zero help. I never got caught up to what I need helpwise.

> I'm constantly hiring. Most of our stores have vacancies all of the time.

Most New York chains hire constantly. One reason for the intense demand for part-time youth is that few stay on the job for any significant period of time. "I have plenty of jobs for youth," noted one manager, "the problem is that I can't retain them." Managers cite annual turnover rates for part-timers of 100 percent or more. Teenagers with one year's seniority are viewed as veterans.

But amid their frantic search for teenage workers, managers had many complaints about this work force. Absence and lateness were chronic and many failed to call in when they did not show up. Theft was reported to be a constant problem.

But despite these complaints, the supermarket industry in New York is relying more and more on a part-time teenage labor force. Managers reported that during the first half of the 1980s, they had moved from a predominantly full-time labor force to one that was 60 to 70 percent part-time. This trend appears to result from four factors: (1) the increasing differential between wages for full-time and part-time workers; (2) increases in store hours; (3) changes in consumer tastes; and (4) new technological developments.

At least in New York, rising wages for full-time adult workers appear to be driving the stores toward growing utilization of youth. Hourly wages for a full-time cashier are more than $10 an hour, and fringes are over 35 percent of the hourly wage. In addition, labor costs rise sharply for any overtime involved. Full-time workers employed after 6 P.M. receive premium pay. Part-timers are seen as the solution to these high labor costs. The attraction of part-timers is that they can be paid the minimum wage with substantially lower fringe benefits. Moreover, since the last increase in the minimum wage in 1981, wages for full-timers have risen annually; therefore, the differential between full-timers and part-timers has widened.

Two additional factors have strengthened the demand for teenagers. First, as in the fast-food restaurant sector, evening and weekend shifts, which require large numbers of part-timers, have expanded significantly over the past decade. A second stimulus results from changes in consumer buying habits. For example, many consumers also have a preference for selecting their own produce, rather than purchasing produce packaged in bulk by the stores. Satisfying these tastes means reverting to the traditional grocery store practices that predated the supermarket. Although this trend has given rise to trendy food boutiques and small greengrocers, the chains have restructured their operations to meet the demand for this type of labor-intensive service. This in turn has led to an expansion of the supermarket labor force.

As we have seen, the shift toward part-time employment is by no means problem-free and the costs of constantly hiring and recruiting part-timers are high. Yet store executives were emphatic about the savings provided by part-time labor: "It would simply cost us too much in salary and fringes to move to an entirely full-time labor force." And the part-time, high-turnover characteristics of teenage workers offer a very flexible labor force: Schedules can be changed, expanded, or shrunk on short notice.

Although immigrant employment in the industry has also grown, it is interesting that supermarket operators have not turned to older immigrants to solve their turnover and other personnel problems. Language problems are perhaps one explanation, but as was the case with fast-food outlets, the part-time and short-term labor market attachments of teenagers fit well with the supermarket labor process, which has evolved in such a way as to minimize the disadvantages of high turnover.

In another parallel with restaurants, the immigrants who are moving into the retail food industry are concentrated in a fast-growing sector of small immigrant-owned grocery stores that depend on more stable adult workers. According to the Korean Produce Retailers Association, there were about 1,600 greengrocers in New York in 1984, most of whom had opened within the previous five years. Of the 1,600, about 900 were owned by South Koreans.[29] Rather than recruiting from the general labor market, as do the supermarkets, these firms are organized around family ties and ethnic labor. By utilizing the entire family they both lower labor costs and maintain control and flexibility in the work process. As Illsoo Kim has noted in his work on Korean immigrants:

> Korean storekeepers can maintain long store hours without paying overtime wages. Furthermore, they rarely observe the various American holidays, and, since their employees are family members, they do not pay holiday wages. By thus cutting labor costs, Korean retail businesses reduce overall costs and are able to compete with supermarket and chain-store prices. The statement by a Korean businessman, "In this business you can earn only labor costs" means to Korean immigrants that, if they do not have any specific skills that are salable in the United States market, they might better employ themselves and their family-members in labor-intensive businesses.[30]

This system has also influenced the behavior of the supermarkets. One manager stated: "In order to compete with them [the Koreans] we have shifted our produce department to a bulk produce operation and have also been offering higher quality produce. However, the result of this is that our labor costs increase." The same manager stated that a supermarket in his chain lost produce sales to a Korean fruit and vegetable store located nearby.

Whereas the growth of Korean and other immigrant businesses has thus reduced the supermarkets' share of the industry and indirectly, the demand for teenage labor, immigrant businesses themselves hire few teenagers. Given a supply of older immigrant workers, who comprise a highly reliable, motivated, and cheap source of labor, the incentives to hire youth are diminished. Moreover, the importance of maintaining control over the labor force strengthens the preference for family or ethnic labor and deters Koreans from employing natives, as the following quote from the president of the Korean Produce Retailers Association suggests: "We should be especially cautious in employing

Americans, because union officials may encourage them to become union members. Once they belong to the union, extra expenses such as overtime payments, the hourly minimum wage, and social security taxes follow. Small Korean fruit and vegetable stores cannot afford to pay all these extra costs."[31]   Similarly, restricting employment to coethnics minimizes the costs associated with theft, which, according to supermarket managers, is directly related to the employment of youth.

Nevertheless, it also seems likely that to the extent that immigrant-owned stores, through competition, have pushed the supermarkets toward longer hours and more labor-intensive methods for handling produce, then the growth of the immigrant sector is also partly responsible for the growth of teenage employment in the supermarket. Furthermore, outside of New York or other densely populated cities, the greengrocer phenomenon, which depends on foot traffic, is much weaker. Specialized fruit and vegetable stores are less likely to succeed in suburban shopping malls. Nevertheless, changing demand has pushed supermarkets toward more labor-intensive produce handling, thereby increasing the demand for teenagers even without the accompanying competition from immigrant establishments.

Here we see another similarity to the restaurant case study. An increase in immigrant employment and entrepreneurship in the retail food industry has been accompanied by an increase in teenage employment. Although this increase would have occurred in the absence of increased immigration, and indeed in that case teenage supermarket employment might have risen even more, the supermarket case does illustrate the contrasts between the two groups that differentiate their labor market roles and dampen competition between them.

Contrasting Employment Systems

These comparisons between the employment of immigrants and low-skilled natives illustrate important similarities and contrasts among the labor processes associated with different types of jobs in which the groups are concentrated. For example, both the fast-food and the immigrant sectors serve the low end of the market, using a low-cost labor force that is resistant to unionization and that has the flexibility to adjust to hourly and seasonal fluctuations. In the immigrant sector, the cooking methods are labor-intensive and traditional, skills persist, and menus are large. In the fast-food sector, methods are capital-intensive, skills are eliminated, and the limited fare consists of a few standardized, precooked items. Immigrant restaurants employ full-time (or super-full-time) workers who often make a career in the industry, whereas fast-food outlets hire part-timers with low commitment to restaurant work. Indeed, fast-food production is made possible by the absence of a career orientation among most of the employees. In the immigrant sector, training is informal and outside social relationships play a central role both in training and hiring. In the fast-food sector, training for lower-level employees is minimal, whereas training for the managers is formally organized. And outside social relationships are not important. Thus immigrants and low-wage natives are concentrated in sectors that use distinct labor processes. In the next chapter, I explore the roots of that differentiation and how it influences the effect of immigration on the employment of native youth and women.

Notes

1. Ivan Charner and Bryna Shore Fraser, *Fast Food Jobs* (Washington, D.C.: National Institute for Work and Learning, 1984).

2. Even in fast-food restaurants there are sharp differences in the jobs held by men and women. Seventy-five percent of the women compared to 29 percent of the men in Charner and Fraser's sample reported that their primary responsibility involved serving customers at a counter or hosting in the dining room, whereas 39 percent of the men (versus 4 percent of the women) were primarily engaged in cooking. Charner and Fraser, 1984, p. 23.

3. Charner and Fraser, 1984, p. 5.

4. U.S. Bureau of the Census, *Census of Population: 1980, Detailed Population Characteristics, United States Summary, PC80-1-D1-A* (Washington, D.C.: GPO), table 253.

5. Daryl D. Wyckoff and W. Earl Sasser, *The Chain-Restaurant Industry* (Lexington, Mass.: Lexington Books, 1978), p. xlviii.

6. U.S. Bureau of the Census, *Census of Business: 1967, Retail Trade Area Statistics, United States* (Washington, D.C.: GPO), table 2; and U.S. Bureau of the Census, *Census of Retail Trade: 1982, Geographic Area Series, United States* (Washington, D.C.: GPO), table 1.

7. Wyckoff and Sasser, 1978, p. 5.

8. Wyckoff and Sasser, 1978, p. 1.

9. According to estimates by the investment banking firm of Salomon Brothers, in 1977, $24 billion of the $64 billion restaurant market was accounted for by 125 chains with sales over $15 million. The twenty-five largest chains had sales of $17.5 billion or 27 percent of the entire market. Most of these chains were in the fast-food sector. In fact, seven hamburger fast-food chains (McDonalds, Burger King, Wendy's, Hardees, Jack-in-the-Box, Gino's, and Burger Chef) accounted for almost 50 percent of total chain sales. Robert L. Emerson, *Fast Food* (New York: N.Y.: Lebhar-Friedman, 1979), pp. 55–60.

10. Charner and Fraser, 1984, chapter 2.

11. Charner and Fraser, 1984, p. 32.

12. Charner and Fraser, 1984, p. 21.

13. Charner and Fraser, 1984, p. 110.

14. The following statement by R. Davis Thomas, chairman of Wendy's Corporation in 1979, vividly illustrates the quest by managers in the industry to simplify work processes and eliminate skills. His statement is a response to a question concerning the competitive impact of the introduction by McDonald's of an additional menu item. "No. They won't be able to do it. They've got too many items. You can't train people to do all these different things. We have a hard enough time just cooking hamburgers and making chili and getting the orders done, let alone adding a steak sandwich on. How many sandwiches have they got now? It's like a state of confusion. They've got a problem. I always knew that problem. I knew that when we were in the food business years ago and we had the same problem. I thought you could eat here for 100 days and not eat the same thing. Why aren't we doing more business? Remember it is not you and me fixing it, it's school kids, their first job. We've got to train them to make sandwiches, to make drinks, to make chili. We have 90 percent of our employees part time. The same thing with McDonald's" (Emerson, 1979, p. 93). Thomas is then asked whether he thinks that success requires "a very simple menu with simple preparation," He responds: "Yes. If I had been with a broad menu operation I wouldn't still be in the business because I hate it that bad. I just learned my lesson about the dishwashers and the waitresses and I just think it is a super tough business" (Emerson, 1979, p. 93).

15. Wyckoff and Sasser, 1978, chapter 5.

16. Charner and Fraser, 1984, p. 29.

17. Emerson, 1979, p. 194.

18. Emerson, 1979, pp. 187–194.

19. N.Y. State Department of Labor, *Earnings and Hours in the Restaurant Industry in New York City*, Wage Bulletin 308 (November 1981) and 334 (November 1983).

20. Roger Waldinger and Thomas Bailey, "The Youth Employment Problem in the World City," *Social Policy* 16 (Summer 1985): 55–58.

21. The dependent variable was the ratio of fast-food sales to sales in all other eating places. These data were from *Census of Retail Trade: 1972.* Immigrants from Western Europe and Canada were not included in the immigration variable. Immigration and demographic data were from *Census of Population: 1970.* The elasticity of the dependent variable with respect to the proportion of the SMSA population accounted for by the foreign born was −.11 with a standard error of .02. See Thomas Bailey, "Labor Market Competition and Economic Mobility in Low-Wage Employment: A Case Study of Immigrants in the Restaurant Industry" (Ph.D. dissertation, Economics Department, Massachusetts Institute of Technology, 1983).

22. U.S. Bureau of the Census, *Census of Population: 1980*, table 287.

23. U.S. Bureau of the Census, *Census of Population: 1980*, table 289.

24. Emerson, 1979, pp. 55–60.

25. The short-term perspective that managers have with respect to training is suggested by the following discussion of training in a textbook for restaurant personnel management. "There's always one objection to training: Many people feel it's useless, since employees come and go so fast. The question of turnover and training is a difficult one to answer. Certainly a trained employee gives you more for your money than an untrained employee. Let's say you hire a dishwasher for one day and spend *30 minutes* training him. If the manager knows how to train effectively, those 30 minutes will pay off the very first day. If the dishwasher stays two days, you've got a bonus. . . .

"Another example: You hire a cook and spend *two hours* training him. You introduce him to your recipes, the ingredients required, and the equipment you use. You spend the rest of the day answering his questions. If he only stays that one day, he did something that left more free time for you. Chances are, he'll stay more than one day. And if he does, the second, third, and fourth days will pay heavy dividends on your training investment. Even with the high turnover that seems to plague every food service operation, trained employees produce more than untrained employees. . . .

"If you're still not certain whether or not to train, consider these comments from managers who took the time to train: 'Trained workers learn faster. I teach my new servers the menu prices in *30 minutes.* It used to take a whole day for them to learn on their own.'" (emphasis added) Neil R. Sweeney, *Managing People: Techniques for Food Service Operators* (New York: N.Y.: Lebhar-Friedman Books, 1976), pp. 66–67.

26. Research has found that firm size is not a good predictor of work satisfaction or other measures that might indicate a personal or family-like work environment. Both Bendix and Newby emphasize that employment can be just as alienating in small firms as in large bureaucratic organizations. Furthermore, Lawson's case study describes the use of paternalism in a large, indeed a multinational, firm. Doeringer does not mention the size of the paternalist firms in his study, but presumably some had more than a few workers. But in both of these cases, the firms had long traditions of close ties to the labor force and in Doeringer's study, were in relatively isolated rural areas. Therefore, despite these exceptions, small firm size is certainly an important characteristic that increases the possibility of developing the personal relationships on which paternalistic personnel practices can be built. See Howard Newby, "Paternalism and Capitalism," in Richard Scase, ed., *Industrial Society: Class, Cleavage and Control* (New York, N.Y.: St. Martins Press, 1977); Tony Lawson, "Paternalism and Labour Market Segmentation Theory," in Frank Wilkinson, ed., *The Dynamics of Labour Market Segmentation* (London: Academic Press, 1981); Reinhard Bendix, *Work and Authority in Industry* (Berkeley, Cal.: University of California Press, 1956); and Peter B. Doeringer, "Internal Labor Markets and Paternalism in Rural Areas," in Paul Osterman, ed., *Internal Labor Markets* (Cambridge, Mass.: MIT Press, 1984).

27. This section on the retail food sector is based on interviews and research conducted jointly by Roger Waldinger and the author. A more detailed report is included in Thomas Bailey and Roger Waldinger, "Marginal

and Out of Work: Youth and Jobs in Post-Industrial New York," unpublished report (New York, N.Y.: Policy Analysis Division, Office of Economic Development of the City of New York, July 1984).

28. U.S. Bureau of the Census, *Census of Population and Housing: 1980, Public Use Microdata Samples (Sample A), New York* (Washington, D.C.: GPO).

29. Lisa Belkin, "For the City's Korean Greengrocers, Culture Often Clashes with the Law," *New York Times,* August 11, 1984, pp. 25, 28.

30. Illsoo Kim, *New Urban Immigrants: The Korean Community in New York* (Princeton, N.J.: Princeton University Press, 1981), p. 113.

31. Kim, 1981, p. 115.

5

Immigrants and
Native Youth and Women

Despite the low skill levels of jobs held by immigrants and by native youth and adult women, comparison among the labor processes in the immigrant, fast-food, and intermediate sectors of the restaurant industry reveals important differences in the types of jobs that these groups tend to fill. In this chapter I shall analyze the underlying influences that shape the labor supply of teenagers, young adults, and women for low-wage jobs, concentrating on the aspects that are relevant to the comparison between the labor market roles of immigrants and the members of each group. In the second part of the chapter material from the case studies as well as other empirical work will be used to discuss the effect of immigration on the employment of native youth and adult women.

The Labor Supply
of Teenagers, Young Adults, and Women

Teenagers

Teenagers dominate the ranks of fast-food workers. Indeed in 1980, 15 percent of all employed teenagers worked in restaurants, and the retail trade industries as a whole accounted for 44 percent of teenage employment.[1] Given the less-than-modest skill requirements of the fast-food production process, teenagers (who of course have not had time to develop skills) are obvious candidates to fill the sector's jobs. But lack of skills is not the only source of the congruence between the characteristics of this group of workers and the sector's labor needs.

Immigrants are also overrepresented in restaurant employment. At first, the concentration of both groups in this industry may appear to result from the low-skill levels that characterize both teenagers and recent immigrants. Similarly, as Michael Piore emphasizes, these groups have a temporary perspective on their employment. [2] For teenagers, restaurant employment is a short-term expedient to be followed by more remunerative activity with higher satisfaction. And for immigrants, the continued indentification with their native countries and lingering plans to return tend to minimize the importance of long-term opportunities associated with their jobs as well as the disadvantages inherent in the low status of restaurant employment.

But a closer look at the restaurant industry's employment pattern suggests that focusing on the similarities, be they in skill level or time horizon, obscures important differences in the labor market roles of the immigrants and teenagers and in the underlying forces that shape those roles. For example, teenagers are concentrated in the fast-food sector, where relatively few immigrants are found. Immigrants, in contrast, dominate the immigrant sector and parts of the full-service sector where youth are not employed. Furthermore, outside of the restaurant industry, immigrants are much less concentrated in retail industries than are teenagers.

One important difference between these groups is the language deficiency of immigrant employees. This becomes an increasing disadvantage for many immigrants as the relative importance of retail tasks increases in the sector. Nevertheless, language problems need not be insurmountable. Frequent restaurant diners in large cities have encountered waiters or waitresses whose English is less than fluent.

For teenagers, employment is associated with a brief stage in the life cycle and is subordinate to other roles and activities. Because families can usually provide basic necessities, the young worker's need for his or her own income is not so urgent as that of a mature worker. Teenage workers therefore not only are unskilled but also tend to be both short-term and part-time workers.

Attendance at high school or college is the most common competing activity, but for many already out of school, employment continues to be a subordinate concern. Paul Osterman argues that, "In the first several years after leaving school young people are frequently in what might be called a *moratorium* period, a period in which adventure seeking, sex and peer group activity are all more important than work."[3]

Employment data indicate that in 1982, 50 percent of all employed workers between the ages of sixteen and nineteen worked part-time, compared to 14 percent for all employed workers. Moreover, this trend in part-time work among teenagers is rising. In 1965, only 41 percent of all teenage workers were employed less than full-time.[4] The part-time workweek of teenagers contrasts to the more than full-time workweeks of immigrants. For example, 73 percent of all male foreign-born but only 37 percent of all sixteen- to twenty-four-year-old native-born restaurant workers in New York reported that they usually worked more than thirty-five hours a week in 1979.[5]

The subordination of work to other activities is also related to lack of job stability. For example, Osterman shows that nineteen-year-old out-of-school youth have only about a 60 percent probability of being employed in the same industry as they were in the preceding year. For sixteen-year-olds, this percentage falls to about 35.[6] Of course, in-school youth are even more unstable than out-of-school youth because the work schedules of the former must conform to the changing rhythm of classes and vacations. Target earning is also common among young workers and is another factor contributing to their instability. This instability also contrasts to tenure levels for immigrants. Restaurant employers reported that they expected immigrants to have longer tenure and to be absent less often than native-born teenagers, a finding also reported in a study of San Diego restaurants.[7]

But as we have seen, the part-time, high-turnover characteristics of the teenage labor force befit the fast-food production process. These characteristics also promote the image that chains want to project: both fast *and* enthusiastic service. Despite low wages, teenagers who view their jobs as temporary can maintain enthusiasm. One manager who was interviewed said that he liked hiring high school students because they got excited by working in uniforms. But enthusiasm for the boring, low-paid jobs in fast-food outlets cannot be maintained over the long term. Among adult workers, it is unlikely that it can be established in the first place. One need only imagine a Burger King staffed by forty-year-old laid-off auto workers to understand how this would change the nature of the industry.

Therefore, whereas teenagers and recent immigrants to some extent share a temporary perspective and a partial commitment to their employment in many low-wage jobs, the social basis of that ambivalent orientation differs between the two groups, a difference that results in the observed divergence in their labor behavior.

To the extent that a primary purpose of immigration is to generate savings or remittances to be used in the home country, the immigrants' objectives are to maximize income and minimize consumption, a goal best met by intensive employment and long workweeks. This contrasts with the case of teenage workers, whose partial labor force commitment results from their involvement in concurrent activities. Because those other activities (attending school, socializing, sports) are more important, their objectives are to minimize the time spent at work.   Therefore, despite sharing low skills and a temporary perspective, immigrants suppress nonemployment activities, whereas teenagers minimize work.

Given these contrasts and the nature of the fast-food production process, the preference for teenage workers becomes clear. The part-time casual goals of teenagers are a better match than the goals of immigrants for the personnel needs of fast-food restaurants. Indeed, as the preferred workers in the sector, teenagers benefited from the sector's expansion during the 1970s. In the New York Standard Metropolitan Statistical Area (SMSA), despite the increase in the immigrant share of the population, the teenage share of restaurant employment increased from 9.3 to 13.9 percent over the decade of 1970–1980. This 49 percent increase in the share was greater than the 42 percent national increase in the teenage share of the industry.[8]

Young Adults

The dining rooms of many New York restaurants as well as restaurants in many other cities are staffed by young adults in their twenties. According to the 1980 census, the twenty- to twenty-four-year-old group continued to be significantly overrepresented in the industry.[9] These workers are particularly important in upper-level intermediate and lower-level full-service-sector restaurants. (The most expensive restaurants tend to use older waiters with more experience.)

Analysts of youth employment emphasize that both the employment experience and behavior of young workers change as they enter their early twenties, with unemployment decreasing and job tenure rising.[10] Paul Osterman calls the post-teenage period the *settling-down* stage in contrast to the earlier *moratorium* stage: "Settling-down behavior is characterized by steadier commitment to job and to the labor force. There is less quitting, and average job tenure increases. When unemployed, young men in the settling-down period search more intensively for a job and show much less tendency to drop out of the labor force."[11] Osterman argues that stability grows as this group matures. The probability that an out-of-school white youth will be employed in the same three-digit industry as he or she was in the preceding year rises from about 0.5 to 0.7 between the ages of eighteen and twenty.[12]

Some workers in the twenty to twenty-four age group do seek career employment, but many work in low-quality jobs to support themselves while they are preparing for or at least looking for careers in other industries. These workers are college or graduate students; people actually engaged in another career that does not provide enough income such as actors, actresses, and other artists; or young college graduates who are taking some time to decide what to do next.

Young adults are similar to teenage workers in having competing activities and in viewing their secondary-sector employment as temporary. Although some work full-time, many young adults in low-quality jobs are part-time workers because of commitments to alternative nonemployment activities. Nevertheless, they are more dependable than teenagers both because they are older and because they have a greater need for income than their younger counterparts. Furthermore, the temporary stage with which their secondary-sector employment is associated may last for several years, so that young adults in this group often have greater employment longevity than teenagers.

Therefore, although young adults, like teenagers, are unlikely to put in the more than full-time workweeks that characterize the employment of many immigrants, their dependability and stability on the job results in greater similarities between the employment characteristics of this group and immigrants than between the characteristics of teenagers and immigrants.

But important differences between immigrants and young adults remain. Once again language differences play a role, but for these two groups, differences in social background and socialization are just as important. The availability of young adults for low-quality jobs is partly a result of the schooling extension and the rise in the age of career and family establishment. This pattern is more prevalent in the middle class than in the working class. In the restaurant industry it leads to a seemingly paradoxical situation in which an industry known for its low wages and instability attracts many workers of middle-class origins. On the one hand, young adults are unlikely to be willing to take the worst and lowest-paid dishwashing jobs in marginal restaurants. On the other hand, their socialization makes them an attractive source of dining room workers for restaurants serving a middle- and upper-class clientele.

Moreover, young adults are less likely to provide a source of skilled cooks and entrepreneurs than immigrants. Even if young adults remain in the industry for relatively long periods of time, thereby accumulating experience and skills, they usually continue to have opportunities outside the industry through education or access to employment in industries with better and more secure advancement opportunities. Furthermore, their part-time workweeks minimize the amount of experience and skills that they accumulate in a given amount of time.

To be sure, some young workers do eventually remain in the food-service industry if they find their educational credentials worth less than they had hoped or if incomes from their preferred careers need to be supplemented. Several examples of this were found in the interviews conducted for this project. One steak-house manager had graduated from college with a humanities degree but had found no work in his field. Another manager had a degree in psychology. Both of these workers viewed their restaurant employment as temporary. The general manager of a large New York restaurant had moonlighted in restaurants while employed as a high school English teacher. He finally stopped teaching. Other managers mentioned maitres d'hotel, captains, and full-time, long-term waiters who had started out as waiters to supplement earnings from careers as artists but had gradually devoted more time to restaurant work.

Nevertheless, such developments in the careers of these young people are not planned. Working as part-time unskilled workers in the industry is perfectly consistent with their initial goals with respect to restaurant employment. But according to those goals, becoming a full-time cook represents failure. Restaurant employment is initially a short-term expedient to be followed by a more remunerative activity with higher status and satisfaction. Long-term restaurant employment becomes more attractive only when other opportunities are not forthcoming, that is, when they fail to achieve their initial aspirations.

Women

The employment of women has been much studied recently, but from the viewpoint of this book, the important conclusion to be drawn from research is that women are a primary source of workers who work dependably at low-paying jobs that provide little opportunity for advancement. To be sure, women have made dramatic gains in entry-level positions in the professions, although it remains to be seen how their careers compare to those of men. Nevertheless, the 57 percent increase in the number of female labor force participants during the decade preceding 1981[13] were not all absorbed by high-quality jobs. (Male labor force participants increased by only 34 percent over the same period.) Indeed, women continue to be concentrated in female-labeled jobs, albeit this concentration has fallen slightly over the past twenty years.[14] Although the underlying assumptions of the division of labor have been challenged, the primary homemaking and parental responsibilities remain with women.[15]

Thus as late as 1982, while 25.5 million wives were in the labor force, 21.3 million were out of the labor force because they were "keeping house." Moreover, 20 percent of all adult female labor force participants worked part-time compared to 5 percent for men.[16] And many of the full-timers still view their employment roles as secondary.

This situation may increasingly come into conflict with the occupational aspirations of women, but the transformation of women's attitudes or employment roles does not appear to have been as widespread or as rapid as had appeared likely some years ago. As one analyst concluded, the result is that many low-level jobs are still "performed by women who are neither demanding career opportunities nor seeking to establish themselves in the labor market in the sense implied by the occupational mobility pattern of men."[17]

The occupational distribution of women in the restaurant industry reflects their subordinate position in the economy as a whole. While only 35 percent of the managers in the industry in 1980 were women, they accounted for 88 percent of all waiters and waitresses. About one-half of all female restaurant workers in that year were waitresses, and the better and higher-paying waiting jobs were usually held by men. Moreover, the distribution of occupations among men and women within the industry did not change significantly between 1970 and 1980. Women accounted for about 60 percent of the industry's labor force in both 1970 and 1980. The proportion of managers who were female grew only 5 percentage points, and the female proportion of waiters and waitresses fell only two points over the decade. Even fast-food jobs are gender-typed, with women taking orders and men making the hamburgers. And whereas in 1970, 49 percent of all cooks were female, by 1980 that figure had dropped to 44 percent.[18]

Older women are concentrated in waiting and counter jobs in more humble establishments that are often near their homes. This facilitates part-time work while children are in school and minimizes transportation and time expenses. The place of these restaurants in the life cycle of long-term waitresses was described by Louise Howe in her book *Pink Collar Worker*: "'Diners and coffee shops,' [a waitress] told me, are 'where waitresses often start, where they work while they're raising their kids, and where they return when they're too old for the sexpot jobs.'"[19]

Because of the subordination of their jobs to other roles and the expectations they have about the future opportunities associated with their jobs, waitresses usually continue to maintain a short-term perspective on their employment despite many years of experience. This paradox was revealed in another one of Howe's interviews: "Well, I don't know, I've never stayed on a job that long, and I guess even though I've been doing it so long, I've never really identified myself as a waitress. You can be in it for twenty years and still think it's a temporary thing."[20]

In many ways, the characteristics of the employment of mature women and those of immigrants are similar. In particular, both groups provide stable and dependable labor for low-quality jobs. In both cases, their willingness to take such jobs is rooted in their short-term employment perspective and their ambivalent commitment to the labor market (or at least in the case of immigrants, the host country labor market). But as is the case with teenagers and young adults, the differences in the roots of this ambivalence between native women and immigrants result in differences in the employment roles played by the two groups. In particular, the intensive employment of immigrants during their initial period contrasts with the weaker attachment of women. And if women shift to a stronger commitment, it requires a change in orientation toward work, that is, they become more involved with work and work more hours. A shift to a longer-term commitment on the part of immigrants involves not so much an increased attachment to work, but a change in the social context within which that work is located. Indeed, in contrast to the case with women, this change may involve a reduction in work hours, not an increase.

Moreover, the lengthening of the employment perspective of immigrants takes place in a social context that is often tied closely to the labor market and is intertwined with whatever employment opportunities are available. Thus, the conjuncture of immigrant business and immigrant community provides contacts that can be useful in finding better, but nevertheless related, jobs. The social contacts of native women are less likely to be useful in this way. Their husbands are usually in completely different industries, and if they know other women who work, they are probably also in low-level jobs.

This problem is closely related to gender stereotyping of jobs, which, as we have seen, is severe in the restaurant industry. This stereotyping tends to confine women to female enclaves and also reduces competition for those jobs. For example, in intermediate-sector restaurants, immigrants typically are employed in the "back of the house" while native women serve the food. Thus, even with the abundance of foreign-born workers, there is still a demand for native-born waitresses. Language proficiency is an additional buffer between the groups, although it is interesting to note that in immigrant-owned restaurants there are more waiters relative to waitresses than in comparably priced intermediate-sector restaurants and that serving workers with less-than-full command of English are common.

It was argued earlier that immigrants play a dual role in the labor market: On the one hand, they dependably fill low-quality entry jobs, but on the other hand, they provide a labor supply for certain types of skilled jobs that are more or less attached to those entry positions. In contrast, women compete only with respect to the first of these roles, and even here the competition, at least with immigrant men, is mitigated by gender stereotyping and language deficiencies.

Finally, differences between immigrants and other workers that are most obvious outside of the restaurant industry may still influence the interactions among the industry's groups of workers. In 1980, nationally, about 6 percent of all employed women worked in restaurants, but in some areas they were more dependent on this industry than on others. Thus in New York City only 2.5 percent of all employed women were restaurant workers.[21] In big cities, many women find employment in the large business and financial service sectors. In particular, the cities that are among the most popular immigrant destinations—New York, Los Angeles, San Francisco, Chicago, Houston, and Miami—are the most important national and regional centers for the business service and finance, insurance, and real estate (FIRE) industries that employ many women in white-collar jobs.[22] Thus, while about 6.5 percent of all employed women in the United States worked in the FIRE sector, over 13.5 percent worked in this sector in the New York SMSA. The employers in these sectors are much less likely to hire recent immigrants. Therefore, although adult women and recent immigrants show important characteristics that should promote competition between them, the contrasting forces that shape their labor market commitments, the structure of the economies in large cities, and differences in language skills, which are particularly important in the service sector, combine to mitigate the potential conflict.

The Impact of Immigration

Many immigrants, teenagers, young adults, and women share the characteristics of low skill levels and a temporary or ambivalent commitment to low-quality employment. This is one reason why these workers all provide a labor supply for the restaurant industry and low-wage employment in general. Whereas the short-term perspective and part-time schedules of the restaurant work force minimize the disadvantages of restaurant jobs, they also reduce the chance that native-born workers will provide a future source of skilled workers and entrepreneurs. In contrast, immigrants, despite their early ambivalence, are more likely to stay in low-wage industries and provide an experienced cadre. In general, the factors that establish tenuous labor force attachment differ between immigrants and native groups, and these factors channel the members of each group into different roles within the overall low-wage labor market.

Even if immigrants and low-skilled natives play different labor market roles, it is possible that they compete: Distinct factors of production can be substitutes. One implication of the foregoing discussion is that it is unlikely that an enduring and general answer to the question of whether immigrants and natives compete can be found. It depends on the characteristics of the immigrants, technological developments, demographic changes, changing tastes, as well as market conditions. The rest of the chapter draws on my argument in this book and on other research to examine the impact of immigration on the employment of native youth and women.

Teenagers

The significant deterioration of teenage employment over the past two decades has coincided with the resurgence of immigration that began in the mid-1960s. Teenage unemployment has been particularly severe in large cities, and over the same period, urban areas have increasingly become the destination of foreign-born newcomers. Although this juxtaposition suggests that immigration has been a major factor in the increase of teenage unemployment, there is reason to doubt the strength of this assertion. First, teenagers and adult immigrants are far from perfect substitutes. Perhaps it is obvious that many of the jobs filled by the foreign born would not go to teenagers if immigration were effectively restricted. The garment industry could hardly depend primarily on teenagers. Teenagers are avoided even for many unskilled jobs, such as those in full-service restaurants. But the case studies in this book have also revealed that teenagers are the preferred work force in fast-food outlets and supermarkets. These jobs are usually in firms that combine modern technology and management techniques in order to allow efficient operations with high turnover. Such firms also have a need for many part-timers for scheduling purposes.

Furthermore, a more detailed examination of changes in teenage employment in New York City over the decade indicates that teenagers have suffered their biggest losses in communication, finance, insurance, and real estate, industries that did not hire large numbers of low-skilled immigrants.[23] Employment in many occupations previously held by teenagers, such as telephone operator, low-level clerk, and filing clerk, have been reduced as a result of technological advances rather than intragroup competition.

Only one quantitative study directly addressed the competition between immigrant and young native-born workers.[24] This study, which is based on 1970 data, considers the competition between eighteen- to twenty-four-year-old black males and suggests tentatively that immigrants and young black males are complements, not substitutes.[25]

Moreover, the decline in the relative teenage share of the population will further reduce the possible conflict between the groups. Although as Vernon Briggs points out, within that shrinking group, the share of inner-city minority teenagers, who experience the most severe labor market problems, continues to grow.[26]

As part of the continuing attempts to understand this problem, research focusing directly on the impact of immigration on this group is essential. Despite the plausibility of the notion that immigration restriction would be an effective policy tool to strengthen teenage employment, the available evidence that we do have simply does not support the conclusion at this time.

Women

One of the most remarkable features of the functioning of the U.S. economy over the past fifteen years has been the absorption of large increases in female labor force participants. In the decade ending in 1984, female employment rose 38 percent, compared to an increase of 11 percent for men.[27] Moreover, during the recession years of 1982 and 1983, the male unemployment rate actually exceeded the female rate.[28] Although female unemployment remains a problem, in contrast to teenagers, for whom high unemployment rates are the focus of policy discussion and design, the important policy issues for women have revolved around the continuing disparity between male and female wages and occupational attainment (even after controlling for age and education) and the burgeoning problems of the feminization of poverty and the presumably associated growth in female-headed households. These issues are viewed more as social problems rather than as labor market problems. Even those who are skeptical about the argument that the wage gap results primarily from discrimination suggest that the gap persists because women continue to shoulder the heaviest child-care and housework responsibilities.[29]

But the influence of immigration on the wage gap or the division of labor between the sexes has not been a prominent issue in policy debates. Indeed, the availability of immigrants to serve as nannies, babysitters, housecleaners, and providers of other services that substitute for housework may be an important factor in relieving native women of some of these chores and thereby promoting their employment and wage gains.

The feminization of poverty also has not been linked to immigration, although at least an indirect argument could be made that the two are related. If immigration reduces the labor market opportunities for minority men and women, it could be argued that immigration promotes economic conditions that weaken the family and lower the income of the female family-heads who do seek employment. Nevertheless, the more direct causes of the problem, such as teenage pregnancy and higher divorce rates, have received more attention. Moreover, the general perception that the labor market differences between black and white women are smaller than those differences between black and white men has probably reduced the focus on the direct labor market problem for black women and, therefore, on the labor market problems that might result from immigration.

Although a concern about the effect of immigration on the employment of women has been overshadowed by discussion about the possible negative effects on other groups, there is evidence that immigrants compete with adult females. Both groups supply dependable labor for low-skilled jobs with restricted opportunities for economic mobility. Competition between women and immigrants in the restaurant industry appears to be more direct than the competition between teenagers and immigrants. To begin with, the difference in the representation of women in the industry in New York and their representation nationally is at least consistent with the hypothesis that immigrants displace women. As we have seen, in 1980 while women over the age of nineteen accounted for 42.7 percent of the industry's work force in the United States, they accounted for only 28.8 percent in the New York SMSA.[30] At the same time, over one-half of the restaurant workers in New York were adult men, although less than one-fifth of the nation's restaurant workers were male. Because many of these adult male workers are immigrants, it appears that without the supply of immigrants, the demographics of New York's industry would be much more similar to those for the nation. Moreover, the roles of the two groups in the industry have important similarities. Women dominate the intermediate sector in the United States, whereas immigrants dominate the sector's work force in New York. And it is the intermediate sector that competes most directly with the immigrant sector. Once again, this is suggested by the contrast between New York, where the intermediate sector accounts for approximately 15 percent of the industry's establishments, and the nation as a whole, where it accounts for about 40 percent.

George Borjas has analyzed directly the impact of immigration on the employment of women.[31] He used a production function framework, which assumes that different demographic groups can be aggregated in various combinations to produce goods and services, to measure the extent of substitutability or complementarity between the groups.[32] Borjas divided the labor force into six groups: native and foreign-born Hispanic males, native and foreign-born white males (all non-Hispanics), black males, and all females. Although Borjas presents many different findings using various assumptions and although the magnitude and statistical significance of the results vary widely with differences in the specification of the estimating equation, his results suggest that immigrants are indeed substitutes for women. These results are particularly strong for non-Hispanic immigrants.[33]

Despite evidence that immigrants and native women are substitutes, the case studies prepared for this book also reveal significant differences between the two groups. As has been shown, even in the intermediate sector of the restaurant industry in New York, women continue to dominate serving jobs while immigrants are concentrated in kitchen jobs. And the low representation of women in the industry in New York is not all attributable to the presence of immigrants. Indeed, New York's large full-service sector and the expense account and luxury demand that it serves is as much responsible for the type of employment in the industry as the characteristics of the labor supply. Moreover, a comparison of data for the decade of 1970–1980 suggests that despite the increase in the city's immigrant population, New York restaurants reduced their dependence on adult men more than restaurants in the rest of the United States did.

These differences between immigrants and native women result from both language deficiency and continued gender stereotyping of some occupations. Moreover, immigrants more than native women are likely to provide a labor supply for skilled and entrepreneurial positions in industries in which the skill-acquisition processes are informal and haphazard. For example, the survival of some segments of the garment industry in New York depends not only on the availability of low-wage workers but also on the social networks to mobilize those workers and to train contractors. Once again, this distinction between women and immigrants results from the different factors that bring these two groups to the low-wage labor market. For the foreign born, these factors are related to the transitional immigration process, whereas for women they emerge from stable social roles.

As was the case for teenagers, broader economic developments may be reducing any possible negative impact on female employment. The burgeoning of the female-intensive white-collar and service industries in the major cities and the opening of professional jobs to women have absorbed many native women who might otherwise have been displaced from lower-level manufacturing and service industries by competition from immigrants.

Notes

1. U.S. Bureau of the Census, *Census of Population: 1980, Detailed Population Characteristics, United States Summary*, PC80-1-D1-A (Washington, D.C.: GPO), table 289.

2. Michael Piore, *Birds of Passage: Migrant Labor and Industrial Societies* (New York, N.Y.: Cambridge University Press, 1979), p. 89.

3. Paul Osterman, *Getting Started: The Youth Labor Market* (Cambridge, Mass.: MIT Press, 1980), p. 11.

4. U.S. Bureau of the Census, *Statistical Abstract of the United States: 1984* (Washington, D.C.: GPO, 1984), p. 410.

5. Sixty percent of the sixteen- to twenty-four-year-old immigrants reported normally working at least thirty-six hours a week during 1979. U.S. Bureau of the Census, *Census of Population: 1980, Public Use Microdata Samples (Sample A), New York* (Washington, D.C.: GPO).

6. Osterman defined industry as a three-digit category in the Standard Industrial Classification. There are hundreds of three-digit industries (forty-two in retail trade alone). Typical retail three-digit industries include grocery store, dairy product store, and eating and drinking place. Osterman, 1980, p. 10.

7. Joseph Nalven and Craig Frederickson, *The Employer's View: Is There a Need for a Guestworker Program* (San Diego, Cal.: Community Research Associates, 1982).

8. U.S. Bureau of the Census, *Census of Population and Housing: 1970, Public Use Samples of Basic Records (5 percent Sample), New York* (Washington, D.C.: GPO); and U.S. Bureau of the Census, *Census of Population: 1980, Public Use Microdata Samples.*

9. While twenty- to twenty-four-year-olds accounted for 14 percent of the employed labor force in 1980, they held 20 percent of the restaurant jobs. See U.S. Bureau of the Census, *Census of Population: 1980*, table 289.

10. Marcia Freedman, *Labor Markets: Segments and Shelters* (Montclair, N.J.: Allanheld Osmun, 1976), chapter 4.

11. Osterman, 1980, p. 18.

12. Osterman, 1980, p. 10.

13. U.S. Department of Labor, *Employment and Training Report of the President: 1982* (Washington, D.C.: GPO, 1982), table A-4.

14. Julianne M. Malveaux, "Moving Forward, Standing Still: Women in White Collar Jobs," in Phyllis A. Wallace, ed., *Women in the Workplace* (Boston, Mass.: Auburn House Publishing Co., 1982).

15. Clair Brown, "An Institutional Model of Wives' Work Decisions," *Industrial Relations* 24 (Spring 1985): 182–204.

16. U.S. Bureau of the Census, 1984, pp. 410, 413.

17. Freedman, 1976, p. 91.

18. U.S. Bureau of the Census, *Census of Population: 1980, Subject Reports, Occupation by Industry,* PC 80-2-7C (Washington, D.C.: GPO), table 4; and U.S. Bureau of the Census, *Census of Population: 1970, Subject Reports, Final Report, Occupation by Industry,* PC(2)-7C (Washington, D.C.: GPO), table 4.

19. Louise Kapp Howe, *Pink Collar Worker* (New York, N.Y.: Putnam's 1977), p. 125.

20. Howe, 1977, p. 125.

21. U.S. Bureau of the Census, *Census of Population: 1980, Subject Reports,* table 1; and U.S. Bureau of the Census, *Census of Population: 1980, Detailed Population Characteristics, New York,* PC 80-1-D34 (Washington, D.C.; GPO) table 122.

22. Thierry Noyelle and Thomas Stanback, *Economic Transformation in American Cities* (Totowa, N.J.: Rowman & Allanheld, 1984).

23. Roger Waldinger and Thomas Bailey, "The Youth Employment Problem in the World City," *Social Policy* 16 (Summer 1985): 55–58.

24. George Borjas, "The Demographic Determinants of the Demand for Black Labor," in Richard B. Freeman and Harry J. Holzer, eds., *The Black Youth Employment Crisis* (Chicago, Ill.: University of Chicago Press, 1986), pp. 191–230.

25. The analysis of competition between black youth and immigrants is a minor part of the study by Borjas, 1986.

26. Vernon M. Briggs, *Immigration Policy and the American Labor Force* (Baltimore, Md.: Johns Hopkins University Press, 1984), chapter 8.

27. U.S. Department of Labor, Bureau of Labor Statistics, *Employment and Earnings* 32 (January 1985), table A-2.

28. U.S. Department of Labor, January 1985, table A-3.

29. Jacob Mincer, "Intercountry Comparisons of Labor Force Trends and of Relative Developments: An Overview," *Journal of Labor Economics* 3 (January 1985 Supplement): S1–S32; and Gary S. Becker, "Human Capital, Effort, and the Sexual Division of Labor," *Journal of Labor Economics* 3 (January 1985 Supplement): S33–S58. Becker argues that lower wages for women result from female specialization in housework, but he does state that he is unable to come up with a market explanation for why women and not men specialize in housework (p. S56).

30. U.S. Bureau of the Census, *Census of Population: 1980, Detailed Population Characteristics, New York,* table 122.

31. Borjas, 1986.

32. The magnitudes of these relationships are measured by the partial elasticity of complementarity that indicates the percentage change in the wages of one group that would result from a 1 percent change in the quantity of another group, holding constant the quantities of all of the other groups (and any other relevant factors of production). Thus if the quantity of immigrants rises, then the demand for those groups that work in conjunction with immigrants will rise; but since the quantity of those groups has not changed, then the increased demand will result in higher wages. If the groups are substitutes for each other, however, then an increase in the quantity of one group will decrease the demand and therefore the wages of the other group.

Borjas estimated factor demand equation for the labor of various demographic groups derived from a production function. In his demand equation, the dependent variable is the individual wage or earnings and the independent variables include measures of the share of the population accounted for by each demographic group (he restricted his sample to eighteen- to sixty-four-year-olds).

33. The Borjas analysis also indicates substitution between females and both young and old black males. The substitution between women and young workers is also revealed in other studies of the interaction among demographic groups. James H. Grant and Daniel S. Hamermesh, "Labor Market Competition among Youths, White Women and Others," *Review of Economics and Statistics* 63 (August 1981): 354–360; and OECD, "Do Relative Wage Levels Affect Youth Employment," *OECD Economic Outlook* (September 1984): 69–86.

6

Formal and Informal Labor Market Processes: Native-born Black Men

The past two decades have seen significant economic gains for native-born blacks. Income, educational levels, and occupational attainment have all risen, but serious problems persist. The gap between black and white earnings even after taking account of differences in education and age has not been eliminated. The labor force participation rate for adult black males has actually decreased over the past ten years, and there appears to be an increasing disparity between educated middle-class blacks and black high school dropouts who never secure a firm hold on the labor market.[1] Even the success of well-educated blacks appears to be unusually dependent on public-sector employment.[2]

What effect has immigration had on the persistence of the economic problems of blacks? The resurgence of immigration after 1965 coincides with the legal and institutional changes that helped bring about the gains that blacks have experienced, and perhaps those gains would have been greater had immigration been restricted. Once again, we return to the restaurant industry to address this question by comparing the roles of black men and immigrants.

The Restaurant Industry

Given the concentration of black men in manual and low-skilled jobs in general, it is surprising to find that they are underrepresented in the restaurant industry. In 1980, black men accounted for only 8.1 percent of employed male restaurant workers while representing 10.7 percent of all male labor force participants. In New York City, black males were also underrepresented, accounting for only 7 percent of male employment. Immigrants, in contrast, were overrepresented in the restaurant industry, comprising 55 percent of the industry's labor force while accounting for 24 percent of the city's enumerated population.[3]

In New York, many black teenagers are employed in the fast-food sector in black neighborhoods as well as in commercial and other nonresidential areas. Nationally, black teenagers are overrepresented among fast-food workers, accounting for 16 percent.[4] Blacks are also managers and franchisees in the fast-food and intermediate-sector chains, whereas black managers are rare in other full-service sectors. In fact, of the eighty-one restaurants in the interview sample no native-born blacks managed restaurants other than fast-food establishments and intermediate chain outlets.

But black access to the ranks of managers and franchisees in the fast-food sector has never been easy. In 1969, there were only five black franchisees in the McDonald's chain. But late in that year, resentment toward the white ownership of four McDonald's outlets in Cleveland's black community resulted in mass demonstrations and a boycott of the stores, and prompted a radical change in the company's franchise practices. Within two years, fifty McDonald's were owned by blacks. Since then black ownership of fast-food operations in the inner city has expanded.[5]

Blacks still face serious barriers; black ownership of suburban stores is much less common. Furthermore, the policy of recruiting fast-food management trainees from outside the hourly work force prevents young blacks from taking advantage of opportunities in the sector's management ranks. This suggests that the black managers and owners in the sector may have acquired these positions through educational credentials or the accumulation of savings outside of the industry. Nevertheless, black representation among both employees and owners in the fast-food sector is stronger than in other sectors of the restaurant industry.

The overall differences between immigrants and blacks are reflected in the occupational distribution of the two groups shown in Table 6.1. Adult black men in the industry were much less likely to be managers, waiters, or cooks than immigrants who had been in the country at least five years. These are the three core occupations in the industry and they account for 70 percent of all male immigrant employment but only 47 percent of all native black male restaurant employment. On the other hand, blacks were more likely to be counter workers and janitors. Even among the cooks, blacks were more likely to be found in the lower-skilled jobs such as short-order cooks.

TABLE 6.1
Percentage Distribution of Native-born Black and Immigrant Males
in the Restaurant Industry, by Occupation, New York City, 1980

| | Foreign-born Males | | | Native-born Black Males | | |
| | Year of Immigration | | | Age | | |
Occupation	1976–1980	1971–1975	Pre-1971	16–24	25 and Older	All Workers
Manager	15	21	27	9	16	21
Waiter	19	14	23	9	10	17
Cook	32	33	23	34	17	22
Bartender	1	2	5	4	10	8
Counter-worker	2	1	3	11	4	4
Janitor	4	3	2	11	7	4
Other	27	26	17	23	35	23
Total	100	100	100	100	100	100

Source: U.S. Bureau of the Census, *Census of Population: 1980, Public Use Microdata Samples (Sample B),* New York (Washington, D.C.: GPO).

The results of the restaurant survey conducted in 1981 for this book are consistent with these census data. Black waiters in New York restaurants were rare. Several managers said that they preferred not to hire black waiters. Two asserted that customers complained if there were too many blacks working in the dining room. Most native-born black men in the survey were working in middle- to upper-level kitchen jobs: short-order cooks, broilermen, general cooks. These jobs can be attained without formal training. Few blacks were found in the lowest kitchen jobs.

Another difference between blacks and immigrants is in the incidence of self-employment (Table 6.2). Although there are many immigrants in lower-level jobs in the industry, 16 percent of these who had been in the United States for at least ten years compared to 12 percent of the adult black males were self-employed.

And the 1981 survey results showed a more striking difference. Of the thirty-five Manhattan restaurants with ten or fewer employees in the sample provided by the New York State Department of Labor, none was owned by a black. Only two of the 156 restaurants in the telephone survey were owned by native-born blacks, whereas about two-thirds were owned by first-generation immigrants.

The underrepresentation of black waiters provides an illuminating example of the position of blacks in this industry. With the possible

TABLE 6.2
Percentage Distribution of Native-born Black and Immigrant Males
in the Restaurant Industry, by Class of Worker, New York City, 1980

Class of Worker	Foreign-born Males Year of Immigration			Native-born Black Males Age		All Workers
	1976–1980	1971–1975	Pre-1971	16–24	25 and Older	
Wage, salary	96	93	84	100	88	90
Self-employed	4	7	16	0	12	10
Total	100	100	100	100	100	100

Source: U.S. Bureau of the Census, *Census of Population: 1980, Public Use Microdata Samples (Sample B), New York* (Washington, D.C.: GPO).

exception of a small number of chefs, waiters in full-service restaurants are the highest paid nonmanagerial employees in the industry. At the time of the 1981 survey, full-time waiters in busy or expensive restaurants often made $500 a week. One manager reported that some of his waiters made as much as $1,000 a week, although they often worked up to sixty hours. This is even more remarkable because a substantial part of the earnings are, in practice, tax free. Furthermore, waiters with longer tenure often have the opportunity to move up to higher occupations such as captain, maître d'hôtel, and manager. To be sure, some waiting jobs require developed skills; nevertheless, this does not appear to justify the high earnings for these jobs. Surely cooking skills are more demanding, yet waiters often earn more than cooks.[6]

Thus, in terms of the relationship between skill requirements and earnings and subsequent mobility opportunities, waiting jobs appear to be more desirable than jobs in the "back of the house." This disparity is reflected in the labor supply for the two types of jobs. Whereas managers of full-service restaurants often complained about the scarcity of skilled kitchen workers, no such complaint was voiced about the supply of waiters and waitresses. Managers of full-service restaurants reported that for every job opening, they had dozens of applicants. There is also a sharp ethnic and social-class distinction between the "back-of-the-house" and the "front-of-the-house" labor force. As the owner of an expensive steak house put it, "My food is cooked by Hispanics and blacks and served by Jews and Gentiles."

In light of the relative desirability of dining room or front-of-the-house jobs, the evolution of the work force that fills these positions is particularly revealing with respect to both the role of immigrants in the industry and the competition between immigrants and native-born minorities, particularly blacks. Expensive restaurants still employ career waiters who have had either considerable experience or formal training, mostly acquired in Europe. As is the case of European chefs, the supply of European-trained waiters has been shrinking over the past twenty years. But the decreased supply of immigrants for waiting positions did not open up these relatively attractive opportunities to blacks. And for that matter, European immigrants have not been replaced by newer arrivals. To a large extent, these jobs now go to young, white, middle-class adults who are also important as a labor supply for the intermediate sector. This group includes actors, actresses, dancers, artists, students, and young people who come to New York looking for work of various kinds. Middle-class behavioral traits as well as the social skills that they acquire as performers and artists make this group of workers, from the viewpoint of the restaurateur, a desirable and adaptable source of waiters for full-service restaurants. Their fluctuating schedules and desire for part-time work provide the flexibility that restaurateurs seek in filling these positions. Thus adult blacks did not get these jobs when the supply of immigrants declined. Immigrants, nevertheless, have access to waiting jobs in immigrant-owned restaurants.

The historical pattern of black employment in the restaurant industry in New York also offers a more general example of the contrast between the roles of black men and immigrants. Both the restaurant and the garment industry case studies suggest that immigrants play a dual role in these industries: They provide low-wage labor, but they move into more skilled and entrepreneurial slots. A typical pattern would be initial employment as unskilled workers and subsequently a greater concentration at higher levels of the occupational hierarchy.

New York's black community has also been a migrant community. Indeed, Michael Piore has drawn a parallel between foreign migration and black internal migration. According to this argument, both blacks and immigrants were willing to take low-quality jobs because of their continued attachment to their home communities. Moreover, the period of migration was demarcated by the severing of that attachment and the establishment of a northern and urban frame of reference for the black community. At this point, blacks became more resistant to low-quality, secondary-sector jobs that no longer benefited from the comparison to even worse opportunities in the South.[7]

But the historical employment patterns of blacks and immigrants in the restaurant industry are not similar. Table 6.3 presents data for the percentage of employment accounted for by restaurants for all workers and for blacks in the New York Standard Metropolitan Statistical

Area (SMSA) for the four censuses between 1950 and 1980. The index of representation provides a measure of the relationship between the employment of blacks in the industry relative to the employment of all workers in the industry. Thus, for example, the index takes a value of 100 in 1960, when 3.6 percent of both all employed men and all employed black men worked in restaurants. Values less than 100 indicate underrepresentation in the industry.

During these three decades, there was an even and secular decline in the representation of black males. Interestingly, this decline was greatest during the 1950s when the immigrant percentage of the city's population was still falling. Even in 1950, when black male representation in the industry in the New York SMSA was at its highest point, only 5.6 percent of all employed black men worked in the industry while in 1970, 8.9 percent of all male foreign-born labor force participants in the SMSA were restaurants workers. Moreover, this figure would be higher for immigrants from developing countries

TABLE 6.3
New York SMSA Employment Accounted for by Eating and
Drinking Places for All Employed Male and Black Male Workers,
Selected Years, 1950–1980

	1950	1960	1970	1980[b]
Male workers, percent of total	4.3	3.6	3.2	4.4
Black male workers, percent of total	5.6	3.6	2.5	2.6
Index of representation[a]	130	100	78	59

[a]The index of representation is calculated by multiplying 100 times the ratio of the percentage of all employed restaurant workers and the percentage of all employed workers. A value of 100 indicates proportionate representation.

[b]The definition of the New York SMSA changed between 1970 and 1980.

Source: U.S. Bureau of the Census, *Census of Population: 1950, Detailed Characteristics, Final Report, P-C31, New York* (Washington, D.C.: GPO), table 83; *Census of Population: 1960, Detailed Characteristics, Final Report, PC(1)-34D, New York* (Washington, D.C.: GPO), table 129; *Census of Population: 1970, Detailed Characteristics, Final Report, PC(1)-34D, New York* (Washington, D.C.: GPO), table 184; *Census of Population: 1980, Detailed Population Characteristics, Final Report, PC80-1-D34, New York* (Washington, D.C.: GPO), table 228.

and Southern Europe because Eastern and Western European workers were underrepresented in the industry. In 1970, representation in the industry among even those immigrants who had been in the country for at least ten years was 6.7 percent. This was more than twice the comparable figure for blacks.[8]

During the initial stages of immigration both blacks and many of the foreign born fill low-quality jobs that nevertheless compare favorably to opportunities in the sending countries or regions. But this is only one of two roles played by immigrants in low-wage labor markets. It is here that the black and foreign immigrant roles diverge. In the restaurant industry blacks have moved into skilled jobs to some extent, particularly as cooks. But this effect is much weaker among blacks than among immigrants, particularly with respect to managerial and entrepreneurial positions.

Immigrants have been successful relative to blacks in using the industry as more than just an opportunity for entrance into the labor market and a source of low-wage jobs. Blacks looked more to the city's public sector and to large white-collar and professional service firms for occupational mobility.[9] Therefore, restaurant employment for native-born blacks was more closely tied to the transition associated with the early stage of immigration than for the foreign born. As settlement of the community was consolidated, restaurant employment became increasingly less attractive to blacks, and without better opportunities, black representation in the industry quickly fell.

The Construction Industry

In the construction industry there is perhaps a greater chance of conflict between black men and immigrants than in the restaurant industry. Although the majority of food-service jobs may have little appeal for adult black males, the hourly wages in construction trades are high for manual work. In 1986, unionized construction workers in New York City earned over $22 an hour.[10] Indeed, there is a history of often militant efforts on the part of blacks to establish themselves in the industry.

Data on the employment of blacks in the construction industry are discouraging. Two decades after the Civil Rights Act, blacks in the United States as well as in New York continue to be underrepresented in construction, and within the industry they remain concentrated in the least skilled occupations. Table 6.4 displays data on black representation in 1970 and 1980 in New York City and the United States. Indeed for the United States, the percentage of the industry's employment accounted for by blacks fell from 8.6 to 7 percent over the

TABLE 6.4
Black Representation in the Construction Industry, New York City
and the United States, 1970 and 1980

	New York City		United States	
	1970	1980	1970	1980
Employed workers				
Percentage black	18.4	22.2	9.5	9.6
Employed construction workers				
Percentage black	15.6	18.1	8.6	7.0
Index of representation[a]	84.8	81.5	90.5	72.9

[a]The index of representation is calculated by multiplying 100 times the ratio of the percentage of all employed construction workers and the percentage of all employed workers. A value of 100 indicates proportionate representation.

Source: Data for New York City are from U.S. Bureau of the Census, Census of Population: 1970, General Social and Economic Characteristics, New York, PC(1)-C34 (Washington, D.C.: GPO), tables 87, 94, 100; and Census of Population: 1980, General Social and Economic Characteristics, New York, PC80-1-C34 (Washington, D.C.: GPO), tables 122, 134, 152. Data for the United States are from U.S. Bureau of the Census, Census of Population: 1970, Subject Reports, Final Report, Industrial Characteristics, PC(2)-7B (Washington, D.C.: GPO), table 33; and Census of Population: 1980, Detailed Population Characteristics, United States Summary, Section A: United States, PC80-1-D1-A (Washington, D.C.: GPO), table 288.

decade, whereas the black share of the total employed work force barely changed. In New York City, the black share of the industry did not grow enough to keep pace with the growth of the black share of total employment. Thus the index of representation for construction fell from 89.6 to 72.9 for construction in the United States and from 84.8 to 81.5 in New York City.

Data for the New York SMSA show improvements in the occupational distribution, but blacks remained underrepresented among the more skilled mechanical trades, such as electrician and plumber, and overrepresented among laborers and the trowel trades such as bricklayer, painter, and plasterer.[11] For example, almost 40 percent of the plasterers and 23.5 percent of the laborers were black.[12]

Whereas blacks are underrepresented in the construction industry, immigrants are overrepresented. In 1970, 29.3 percent of the employed construction workers in New York City were foreign born. By 1980, this share had risen to about 34 percent. This moderate increase is misleading because 84 percent of the immigrant construction workers in 1970 were European; in 1980 the share accounted for by Western Hemisphere immigrants had risen significantly.[13]

The contrasting experience of blacks and immigrants can be better understood by considering the roles of the members of these two groups in the union and nonunion sectors. Over the past twenty years, the nonunion sector has grown rapidly. Recent estimates suggest that open-shop contracts represent about 60 percent of the total construction market and about 25 percent of the commercial construction market.[14] Membership in the most important nonunion employers' organization, the Association of Building Contractors (ABC), has also grown. According to a 1976 survey, ABC membership tripled between 1972 and 1976.[15]

Although in New York the unions have maintained their strength in the construction of large commercial projects in Manhattan, the booming market for additions and alterations has been accompanied by increasing nonunion construction.[16] Although data are incomplete, information collected in interviews by Carmenza Gallo, as well as interviews with Hispanic workers in New York City by Diane Balmori, indicates that the open-shop sector coincides almost entirely with the additions and alterations sector.[17] Very large renovation jobs are probably done by union shops, and new construction, particularly in Manhattan, is entirely carried out by union firms. The main dividing line between the two types of firms seems to be drawn by new and high-rise construction versus rehabilitation. But the dollar volume of construction jobs also sharply differentiates union from nonunion firms. Additionally, nonunion firms tend to be located in the trades that require lower skill levels, such as the trowel trades, painting, and paperhanging, or the skilled but unlicensed trades, such as carpentry.

Blacks have faced barriers both in acquiring training and in securing adequate employment in the construction industry. Any discussion of these barriers focuses almost immediately on the construction unions. This focus is understandable and at least partly justified. The unions' checkered record on integration has been marked by intransigence and thinly disguised, or undisguised, ploys to circumvent equal opportunity laws. Furthermore, the unions administer most of the training programs in the industry, and although their control of the labor supply has eroded, the unions still decide who works on most large-scale commercial and public projects, particularly in northeastern and midwestern cities. But the fragmented and volatile nature of the industry's markets and productive units and the resultant training processes also make it more difficult for blacks to establish themselves in the industry.

In 1982, the industry did about $300 billion in business nationally, and one million construction contractors employed approximately five million workers.[18] Furthermore, the seasonality, uniqueness, and short-term nature of the projects, as well as sensitivity to business cycles, add to the industry's fragmentation and disorganization. These characteristics create the need for a trained work force, but one that is not attached to a particular firm. Only the very largest firms can make stable commitments to a substantial number of workers. Usually a contractor will have a small core of foremen and skilled artisans who are employed more or less full time, but even these workers are periodically laid off. For most workers, the employer's commitment lasts only the length of a specific task. On the one hand, the industry's floating work force and the institutions that deploy it save contractors the cost of paying workers when they are not working, but on the other, it also eliminates any incentives for contractors to provide training. Although the industry needs skilled workers, individual employers can benefit if they let others provide the training. They will eventually have access to the trained workers because artisans are not attached to the employer who provides the training. But if every contractor followed that strategy, no one would be trained.[19]

Because of the portability of skills, training costs have fallen on the worker or the worker's family, for example when the father trains the son. The family relationship overrides the risk of an employer losing his investment in training and eliminates any out-of-pocket training expenses for the trainee. The traditional apprenticeship to an individual artisan is an extension of the paternal system of training.

This system works effectively when there is little distinction between journeyman and contractor—usually when the projects are small. The journeyman can call on friends and acquaintances when jobs are too large to be handled by himself and his apprentices. Therefore, substantial participation in the industry by the members of a particular community requires that contractors have personal contacts within the community. But the requisite skills for success as a contractor usually are learned by working for another contractor. This system creates very strong barriers to outsiders both because the industry's structure encourages contractors to rely on their own family and acquaintances and because of ethnic antagonism and discrimination.

The family training system, however, is less effective for larger jobs. Individual connections are not likely to be adequate to mobilize, according to complicated schedules, the large numbers of specialized craftsmen necessary to complete these jobs. This introduces the need for different types of institutions to carry out the training and mobilization of the work force. The construction trade unions have been the central institutions serving this function. Because all union contractors contribute to the training fund, no contractor runs the risk of paying the cost of training for competitors. At the same time, the union control of the hiring hall encourages the training process in two ways. First, it increases the chances that the young workers who acquire the training will find employment for their new skills, thereby increasing the incentives for them to devote the necessary time and expense. The second reason concerns the role that journeymen play in the training of young workers. Even when apprenticeship programs include formal classroom training, the bulk of the training is provided informally by journeymen on the job sites. If the journeymen believe that their jobs might be threatened by the new workers that they are training, they will be less likely to provide the necessary instruction. The union hiring hall reduces this problem by providing greater security for the established journeymen.

The union is not the only alternative. One possibility is the very large nonunion firm. For example, Clinton Bourdon and Raymond Levitt point out that some large general contractors have introduced innovations "in training and managing a more specialized work force for routine tasks on large-scale industrial projects." They also "operate extensive worker-distribution planning and information systems which permit them to move supervisors, foremen and skilled mechanics among their projects over wide areas. In so doing, they act to 'internalize' the casual labor market otherwise organized by the union hiring hall or business agent."[20]

These same authors also argue that open-shop firms have tried to recreate the union institutions. "Open-shop firms, working through employer associations, are creating and adopting hiring and referral systems, apprenticeship training and even common occupational classifications and wage rates similar to those found in union construction."[21]

But these innovations have not been adopted widely throughout the industry.[22] Bourdon and Levitt conclude that except for specific training with immediate production benefits, training occurs only when it is imposed by formal government or union programs.

The union hiring hall and training systems, therefore, continue to play a central role for large construction projects. And although these formal union systems are more effective for those projects than is the informal family system, there are many similarities. Instead of completely breaking with the family system, the union system incorporates it. Family training remains an effective way of passing on skills, particularly because much of the training still occurs informally on the job. In fact, according to studies by the Business Roundtable, many union members learn their skills and acquire their journeyman status without graduating from a formal apprenticeship training program, and business agents often circumvent the hiring hall and assign jobs directly over the phone.[23]

Therefore, the union structure based on informal ties allows both systems to operate simultaneously. It is clear why craftsmen find this attractive: It projects the family system into an area of the construction market where otherwise it could not operate. But it also perpetuates the barriers to outsiders that are inherent in the industry's informal structure. For example, membership in the operating engineers locals—the possession of a union book—has traditionally been passed from father to son. Training for this trade was mostly informal, and until a 1982 consent decree required that the two operating engineers locals in New York establish a training program, there was no formal training for this trade in the city.[24] Experienced operators passed on knowledge about the various equipment to younger workers. Skills for different types of equipment were picked up by moving among sites as an assistant or oiler on each machine. If the journeyman were willing, the assistant would be given a chance to operate the equipment. The young workers' exposure to the various pieces of equipment was determined by the union official who assigned the jobs.[25] For all of these reasons, it was difficult for an outsider to acquire experience and skill on a range of machines without the *positive* cooperation of the business agent. Moreover, gaining union membership did not guarantee that a worker would not be restricted to operating those pieces of equipment for which the wages were the lowest.

Informal on-the-job training is also a central component of formal apprenticeship programs. Therefore even when minority workers gain admission to these programs, they may find it difficult to acquire the skills. The following account of a black ironworker who entered the union under an affirmative action plan in Philadelphia illustrates how this can happen.

> Like many black craftsmen, he was snubbed by the journeymen who were supposed to provide him with on-the-job training. "The white guys got more help," he says. And at the union hall, the business agents often bypassed blacks when assigning work. "The first three years I didn't have even a year of working time."

> Finally he entered a training program in a shipyard where black workers taught him how to use the torch, enabling him to return to Philadelphia and pass his apprenticeship test.[26]

An administrator appointed by court order to run an apprenticeship program for one New York local that had failed for several years to comply with an earlier consent decree described how the unions circumvented their own rules.

> Contractors would delegate the hiring of many workers to a maintenance foreman who was a member of the same union. So they just bypassed the hiring hall. While the union business agent was sitting there in the hall saying "I don't understand why nobody calls me any more," workers who were part of the buddy system were being hired directly by the contractor. We found that 80 percent of the hires were made outside of the hiring hall.[27]

Discriminatory practices by the union locals are widespread and often blatant, but minorities also face barriers in the open-shop sector. In fact, to the extent that the union codifies nepotistic and discriminatory practices that are only implicit in the informal sector, the effect of the union is to increase the possibilities that those practices can be changed by government action or other institutional means. Therefore, the antidiscrimination suits in the construction industry are brought against the union locals, not the tiny nonunion firms that are often just as discriminatory, if not more so. Indeed, the greatest problems with enforcement where unions are concerned occur when the union system is most like the informal system: when training takes place outside the apprenticeship programs, when the hiring halls are circumvented.

In fact, available data do suggest that blacks have made gains in the union sector. Nationally, black representation in construction unions has also grown. In 1970, only 33 percent of black construction workers were union members compared to 39.8 percent of all other workers. By 1980, the rate for blacks had risen slightly to 34.6 percent, but it had fallen to only 33 percent for other workers. Thus the black unionization rate was above the overall industry rate.[28] And data for the United States indicate that whenever there are differences in minority participation in the two sectors in apprentice programs, they favor the union sector. Statistics compiled by the Department of Labor on union and nonunion apprentices in certified programs show that minority participation, both in relative and absolute terms, is lower in open-shop programs. In 1978, minorities accounted for 21 percent of all apprentices in union programs while they accounted for only 11 percent in nonunion programs. One appreciable difference between the two sectors existed in training programs for operating engineers: In the union sector, minority participation was almost 33 percent; in nonunion firms, it was close to 10 percent. The same data also indicate that the mechanical trades, considered to be among the highest-skilled trades, were more segregated in the nonunion than in the union sector. In 1974, while minority enrollment in apprenticeships in plumbing and the sheet metal trades was 18 and 20 percent in the union sector, it was 7 percent and 11 percent, respectively, in the nonunion sector. And in New York City, the black share of apprenticeship slots went from 11.7 percent in 1972 to 17.4 percent in 1978.[29]

Blacks, therefore, face a number of interrelated obstacles in both the union and open-shop sectors. The fundamental problem is that the industry is structured in such a way that it is extremely difficult for outsiders to establish themselves. The incumbents and their family and personal acquaintances have advantages with respect to access to industry employment and to acquisition of construction trade skills as well as entrepreneurial know-how.   Black workers have found employment in the industry, but their penetration has been concentrated in the least-skilled trades, whereas they remain significantly underrepresented among those individuals with influence and control in the industry—the skilled craftsmen, the union officers, and the construction contractors.

Although blacks appear to have had relatively more success in the formal sectors, existing data indicate that immigrants have a stronger position in the less-formal settings. One suggestive comparison is between the rates of self-employment. Eleven percent of black construction workers in the New York SMSA in 1980 were self-employed, compared to 17 percent for immigrants.[30] And in her interviews with small construction firms in New York, Carmenza Gallo found that although her sample included about equal numbers of firms owned by native blacks, native whites, and immigrants, fourteen of the eighteen firms owned by immigrants were unorganized, and ten of the sixteen firms owned by blacks were union shops.[31]

The union/open-shop distinction is not the only indication of the formality and institutionalization of the firm's production and labor processes. Gallo also divided her sample firms, which were primarily involved with renovation, into those serving (1) large corporations, (2) public and quasi-public institutions (universities, churches, hospitals, etc.), and (3) small businesses and homeowners. The sample firms owned by whites were more or less evenly distributed among these three segments. But over half of the immigrant firms served the residential and small business sectors where informal networks are needed from which to draw clientele and laborers. In contrast, less than one-quarter of the firms owned by native-born blacks primarily served clients in this sector.

Contracts with government or large institutions were more important to black- than to immigrant-owned firms. Three-fourths of the black owners pointed out that government contracts constituted a significant fraction of their business in the past few years, and eight said that government or institutional contracts accounted for more than 80 percent of their business at one time. These contracts were extremely important for only two out of seventeen foreign-owned firms. Black-owned firms also relied much more than immigrant firms on clientele that made special efforts to recruit minority contractors.

Gallo also argued that blacks and immigrants tended to use different paths to reach entrepreneurship. For example, there were differences between the levels of formal education of black and immigrant owners. Whereas two-thirds of the immigrant owners had no more than a high school degree, two-thirds of the black owners had at least some college and one-third had college degrees. Black owners tended to try self-employment after other plans had failed. Immigrant owners were more likely to open a business in order to "work independently." Thus Gallo concludes that "Unlike the blacks, who seemed to go into business *faute de mieux*, immigrants found in their own businesses a pathway to upward mobility. . . . Ownership for blacks, then, seems, in fact, to be a means of maintaining social status rather than a means to upward mobility as it is for immigrants."[32]

The comparison between blacks and immigrants in the construction industry therefore is similar to the comparison in restaurants. In construction, both as workers and as owners, blacks have had more success in gaining access to the more formal and institutionalized sectors of the industry, and even in those sectors, a major problem for blacks is the extent to which informal processes and networks pervade the industry's supposedly rule-bound functioning. In contrast, recent immigrants are found more in the open-shop sector where they appear to be better able than native blacks to use informal contacts and community networks to establish themselves in the industry. The next chapter explores the reasons behind these differences.

Notes

1. Black men have higher unemployment rates and lower labor force participation rates than whites. Whereas 74.5 percent of all white men twenty years of age and older held jobs at the end of 1984, only 65 percent of all black men did. U.S. Department of Labor, Bureau of Labor Statistics, *Employment and Earnings* (January 1985), table A-44. It also appears that this gap has increased over the past fifteen years. In 1970, the comparable figures were 69 percent for blacks and 75 percent for whites. U.S. Bureau of the Census, *Census of Population: 1970, Subject Reports, Final Report PC(2)-6A,*

Employment Status and Work Experience (Washington, D.C.: GPO), table 10. For discussions of the controversy on black economic and labor market progress, see Richard B. Freeman, "Troubled Workers in the Labor Market," Discussion Paper No. 881 (Cambridge, Mass.: Harvard Institute of Economic Research, February, 1982); and Reynolds Farley, *Blacks and Whites* (Cambridge, Mass.: Harvard University Press, 1984).

2. Freeman, 1982.

3. U.S. Bureau of the Census, *Census of Population: 1980, Public Use Microdata Samples (Sample A), New York* (Washington, D.C.: GPO).

4. Ivan Charner and Bryna Shore Fraser, *Fast Food Jobs* (Washington, D.C.: National Institute for Work and Learning, 1984), p. 92.

5. Max Boas and Steve Chain, *Big Mac: The Unauthorized Story of McDonald's* (New York, N.Y.: Dutton, 1976), chapter 11.

6. Why this contrast persists despite the labor supply condition that would be expected to lead to a wage convergence is certainly a challenge to conventional notions of wage determination. Two factors appear to perpetuate this situation. First, the ethnic and class distinction between waiters and cooks may blunt the resentment that might otherwise build up among the kitchen workers. Insufficient language proficiency among some of the immigrant kitchen workers is another possible justification of the difference. The second factor that perpetuates the high earnings for waiters despite an obvious excess supply is that employers have relatively little economic incentive to reduce their earnings. Although employers are required to pay waiters and waitresses a minimum wage of $2.35 an hour, tips, which account for the bulk of the waiters' earnings, are out of the control of the restaurateur. Moreover, because the practice is uniform across the industry, the waiters' earnings do not influence price competition among full-service restaurants. To be sure, an individual owner might gain a small competitive advantage by establishing a policy to reduce tipping; nevertheless, the custom is so well entrenched that the small possible benefits are outweighed by the resentment among the waiters and possibly the clients that such a move would cause.

7. Michael Piore, *Birds of Passage: Migrant Labor and Industrial Societies* (New York, N.Y.: Cambridge University Press, 1979), pp. 160–162.

8. U.S. Bureau of the Census, *Census of Population: 1980, Public Use Samples of Basic Records (5 percent Sample), New York* (Washington, D.C.: GPO).

9. Thomas Bailey and Roger Waldinger, "A Skills Mismatch in New York's Labor Market?" *New York Affairs* 8 (1984): 3–18.

10. *Engineering News Record*, "Wage Rates for Key Building Construction Trades," July 31, 1986, p. 35.

11. U.S. Census Bureau, *Census of Population: 1980, Detailed Population Characteristics, Final Report, PC 80-1-D34, New York* (Washington, D.C.: GPO), table 219.

12. U. S. Bureau of the Census, *Census of Population: 1980.*

13. U.S. Bureau of the Census, *Census of Population: 1970, Public Use Samples of Basic Records (5 percent Sample), New York* (Washington, D.C.:

GPO); and U.S. Bureau of the Census, *Census of Population: 1980, Public Use Microdata Samples.*

14. *Wall Street Journal*, "Merger Wave Brings Changes to the Construction Industry," October 13, 1982, p. 1.

15. Clinton Bourdon and Raymond Levitt, *Union and Open Shop Construction* (Lexington, Mass.: D. C. Heath and Co., 1980), pp. 12, 13, 115.

16. Expenditures on additions and alterations grew about twice as fast between 1950 and 1980 as total construction expenditures. In 1950 additions accounted for less than 10 percent of total construction; by the late 1970s its share had risen to between one-fifth and one-quarter. New York City Division of Housing and Community Revival, "Report of Building Permits Public Construction, 1950–1980."

17. Carmenza Gallo, "The Construction Industry in New York City: Immigrants and Black Entrepreneurs," Working Paper (New York, N.Y.: Conservation of Human Resources, Columbia University, 1983); and Diana Balmori, "Hispanic Immigrants in the Construction Industry: New York City, 1960–1982," Occasional Paper No. 38 (New York, N.Y.: New York University, Center for Latin American and Caribbean Studies, May 1983).

18. Business Roundtable, "More Construction for the Money," A Construction Industry Cost Effectiveness Report (New York, N.Y.: The Business Roundtable, 1983).

19. For descriptions of the construction training process, see Howard G. Foster, *Manpower in Homebuilding: A Preliminary Analysis* (Philadelphia, Pa.: University of Pennsylvania Press, 1974); and Daniel Q. Mills, *Industrial Relations and Manpower in Construction* (Cambridge, Mass.: Harvard University Press, 1974).

20. Bourdon and Levitt, 1980, p. 55.

21. Bourdon and Levitt, 1980, p. 54.

22. According to the Business Roundtable, although the open-shop sector has 60 percent of the construction market, it provides only about 10 percent of the training funds. Business Roundtable, "Training Problems in Open Shop Construction," A Construction Cost Effectiveness Report (New York, N.Y.: The Business Roundtable, 1982). Nonunion apprenticeship programs exist primarily for carpentry, electrical work, and plumbing, and these programs are concentrated in a few states such as North Carolina, Florida, and Maryland. Furthermore, these programs have a higher drop-out rate than the union programs. See Bourdon and Levitt, 1980, p. 73.

23. Business Roundtable, 1982.

24. New York City Office of Construction Industry Relations, "Problems of Discrimination and Extortion in the Building Trades" (New York, N.Y.: Mayor's Office of Construction Industry Relations, 1982).

25. Information from conversations with members of the Operating Engineers Local 825.

26. Steven Askin and Edmund Newton, "Blood, Sweat and Steel," *Black Enterprise* (May 1984).

27. Askin and Newton, 1984.

28. U.S. Department of Labor, Bureau of Labor Statistics, "Selected Earnings and Demographic Characteristics of Union Members, 1970," Report No. 417 (Washington, D.C.:   GPO), table 13, and "Earnings and Other Characteristics of Organized Workers, May 1980," Bulletin No. 2015, (Washington, D.C.: GPO), table 17.

29. David Vander Els, "An Analysis of Apprenticeship Training in the Non Union Sector of the Construction Industry" (Cambridge, Mass.: Department of Civil Engineering, Massachusetts Institute of Technology, 1976); and New York State Department of Labor, *Minority Participation Rates in New York City Construction Industry Apprenticeship Programs, 1972-78* (Albany, N.Y.: New York State Department of Labor, 1979).

30.   U.S. Bureau of the Census, *Census of Population: 1980, Public Use Microdata Samples (Sample B), New York* (Washington, D.C.: GPO).

31. Gallo, 1983.

32. Gallo, 1983, p. 21.

7

Immigrants and Black Men

The contrasts between the roles of black men and of immigrants in the restaurant and construction industries suggest that black men have made their most impressive gains in the more institutionalized and formally organized segments of the labor market whereas immigrants are concentrated in the fragmented and informally organized segments, both as skilled and unskilled workers. This difference is also reflected in the overall economy.

Indeed, the labor market progress of black men has been centered in the public sector, which is very much subject to formal procedures and regulations. Since the 1930s, the various levels of government have been important sources of employment opportunities for blacks.[1] By the early 1960s, black access to upper-level nonmanual jobs was greater in the public than in the private sector.[2] And in 1970, over one-half of black male college graduates were employed by the government, compared to one-quarter of white male college graduates.[3] Between 1960 and 1976, 55 percent of nonagricultural employment growth for black men was in the public sector while only 26 percent of such growth for white men was in government. During the 1960s and early 1970s, upward mobility out of low-level jobs within government was actually higher for black men than for white men.[4] This concentration continued into the 1980s, when only 18 percent of all New York City residents were employed in the public sector, compared to 34 percent of all black workers.

This contrasts sharply with the employment of immigrants whose English language deficiencies alone would make them less likely to work for a public employer. In any case, in 1980 only 8 percent of New York's employed foreign-born population was working in the public sector.[5]

Black dependence on more formal and institutionalized industries extends beyond the public sector. As Freeman concluded, "With respect to blue-collar jobs, perhaps the most positive fact about the current condition of black workers is that they are disproportionately represented in unions and hold a large number of stable high-wage blue-collar jobs."[6] As Chapter 6 indicated, in the construction industry blacks have been more successful in the unionized sectors or in those sectors serving large institutional clients, rather than in the renovation and house-building sectors, which are predominantly unorganized and in which immigrants are employed in large numbers. Jonathan Leonard, in a study of 1,273 California manufacturing plants between 1974 and 1980, found that the employment share of black males increased significantly faster in union than in nonunion plants.[7] In contrast, the foreign born are overrepresented in low-level service and nondurable manufacturing industries.

The scarcity of self-employed blacks in the restaurant industry also reflects the situation in the economy as a whole. In 1980 in New York City, only 3 percent of working black men were self-employed, compared to 12 percent of immigrant males.[8]

Several factors contribute to these differences between black men and immigrants. A temporary or secondary commitment to the labor market is one basis of the "willingness" of recently arrived immigrants, teenagers, and some native women to work in low-quality jobs. This is a perspective not generally shared by native adult males. To the extent that black males are confined to low-quality jobs, it is not because these jobs fit into their other activities or that they plan to return to another country, but because they have only limited access to better alternatives. These circumstances are not likely to promote enthusiasm among young blacks for restaurant careers, for example. Indeed, resentment at being confined to low-status menial jobs, which are so abundant in the restaurant industry, was a primary cause of the civil rights movement and the urban riots of the 1960s.[9]

The immigrants' more favorable perspective on low-wage jobs is also enhanced by the comparison to even worse opportunities in their home countries. For blacks low-quality jobs do not benefit from such a comparison. Therefore, at the least, immigrants are willing to take such jobs at wages below those that would be acceptable to large numbers of native-born adult black males. But the differences are more than ones of perception; immigrants face more favorable opportunities in the informally organized industries dominated by small firms than blacks do.

First, the most common routes of mobility are often closed to first-generation immigrants who arrive with few skills and low levels of education. Language problems, age, and the need for immediate income often foreclose the possibility of using education as a means of upward mobility or as an entry to careers. Access to primary sector job ladders is also restricted. Therefore, over even the long term, immigrants are frequently limited to opportunities available in the secondary-sector industries in which they are initially employed.

Many blacks, in contrast, have found employment in the country's basic industries where they have access to well-organized internal labor markets and job ladders. The overrepresentation of black males in durable goods manufacturing and public administration is evidence of this access. Indeed, blacks who do not have access to employment in basic industries are likely to view secondary-sector jobs with less enthusiasm than immigrants.

Discrimination against blacks also restricts their employment in the retail and service industries in which workers have contact with the public. In the restaurant industry, this affects the hiring of blacks for waiting and other dining room jobs. During field interviews, two managers of full-service restaurants actually stated that they avoided hiring blacks as waiters because of customer preferences. Whether this reflects the clients' or the managers' perspective, the effect on the employment of black waiters is the same. As has been shown, when the supply of European waiters declined during the 1960s, New York's full-service sector did not hire blacks for these relatively high-paying jobs; rather, it turned to the city's supply of artists and actors.

Their limited access to waiting jobs in the restaurant industry also weakens the opportunities for blacks to move up to managerial and entrepreneurial positions. Most restaurateurs who worked their way up had at least some waiting experience. Because waiters' incomes are high relative to their skills and experience, working as a waiter also gives the employee the chance to accumulate the savings necessary to become independent, and when owners of full-service restaurants draw their managers from their employees, they almost always do so from among waiters and bartenders. Hence, because blacks are underrepresented in the better dining room jobs, it is more difficult for them to accumulate the experience and capital necessary for successful entrepreneurship.

Federal government policy over the past twenty years has made progress against the effects of discrimination. Studies of the early years of affirmative action and of equal opportunity enforcement and litigation found at most weak effects,[10] but more recent research has shown that the legal pressure has positively affected black employment.[11] Consolidation of enforcement in the Labor Department in the late 1970s is one reason for this improvement. Thierry Noyelle argues that a shift in Equal Employment Opportunity Commission (EEOC) strategy from a case-by-case approach to one that emphasized class-action litigation against large employers contributed to more effective enforcement.[12] Thus in the early 1970s, EEOC negotiated consent decrees with the American Telephone & Telegraph Company and with nine steel companies[13] in which the firms agreed to establish detailed employment goals as well as specific internal promotion procedures.   These decrees, and others that followed, involved industries dominated by a small number of large employers and a few powerful unions. Thus Noyelle concluded that "Most [of the decrees] dealt with industries in which the discriminating institutions on both the demand and the supply sides of the labor market were easily identifiable and targetable."[14] The importance of identifiable targets is also evident in the restaurant industry, where demonstrations against McDonald's in Cleveland in the early 1970s opened franchises to blacks, and in the construction industry, where blacks have made more progress through the unions than through open shops. EEOC enforcement is a much less effective tool in fragmented and informally organized industries.

Greater reliance on formal rules and institutions by blacks compared to immigrants also results from apparently more restricted or less useful social networks. The immigration process itself selects individuals who are integrated into family and ethnic networks, and these ties are also resources for capital, job finding, skill acquisition, and business relationships. They are particularly important in the fragmented industries that lack organized and predictable structures for skill acquisition and job promotion. Although informal and reciprocal relationships are important among lower-class blacks, these ties appear to be weaker among blacks in the labor force.[15] The ineffectiveness of informal networks among blacks is demonstrated in their unusual dependence on formal labor market intermediaries for job finding.[16] For example, black fast-food workers were more likely than whites or Hispanics to find jobs through employment agencies.[17] And Henry Becher found that in a sample of sixteen- to twenty-four-year-olds collected as part of the *Current Population Survey* in 1973, 15.2 percent of the blacks (compared to only 4 percent of the whites) found that public employment services or community organizations had been the most useful intermediaries in finding their current jobs.[18]

The absence of black-owned businesses is also a labor market handicap for blacks. The presence of the immigrant sector reduces the overall effects of discrimination against immigrants in employment or occupational attainment; foreign-born owners are less likely than their native-born counterparts to discriminate against immigrant workers. In restaurants, this offers opportunities for immigrants to obtain waiting and managerial jobs that are less open to blacks. The lack of black-owned firms deprives blacks of the training and social benefits available to the foreign born in the immigrant sector.[19]

Chapter 3's analysis of the roots of immigrant entrepreneurship suggests why representation in self-employment is so much lower for blacks than for immigrants. The analysis proposes that six factors promote self-employment among immigrants: (1) an investment orientation inherent in the migration process; (2) possible experience in the entrepreneurial-oriented informal sectors of the home countries; (3) initial intensive employment in informally organized small firms in the host countries linked to the limited access to primary-sector jobs; (4) the strength of social networks; (5) privileged access to hard-working low-cost labor; and (6) the training and other advantages associated with employment in the immigrant sector.

The first two factors directly concern the process of immigration and the possible characteristics of the sending economy and therefore do not apply to blacks. The third reason is also rooted in the dynamics of the immigration process and in the adjustments in expectations and orientation that accompany settlement. Networks, too, are stronger among immigrants. If blacks reject low-quality jobs in small businesses or take them without enthusiasm, then black owners have less access than immigrants to a low-wage labor force. And the absence of black-owned sectors is self-perpetuating because potential young black entrepreneurs lack the opportunities for training and experience that immigrants enjoy in ethnic firms.[20]

Thus, the conditions that promote self-employment among immigrants either do not exist or are much weaker for blacks. The large disparity in the incidence of entrepreneurship between these two groups follows from the differences in the social contexts that shape their participation in the labor force. In particular, I have emphasized the role that the immigration process itself plays in the development of immigrant business.[21]

Black progress has resulted more from political organization and general political pressure than from economic organization within the black community. But political pressure is more effective in some sectors of the labor market than in others. It is precisely the industries characterized by small firms and by informal production and labor processes that are farthest from the reach of the government and the various formal labor market institutions. Thus for blacks, working in an entry-level job in these industries is, in effect, a worse investment than it is for immigrants. The opportunity costs and the social costs (the status associated with the job) are higher, the process of skill acquisition more haphazard, and the expected payoff lower.

The Impact of Immigration

Immigrants and native blacks are concentrated in different industries and in different industrial sectors. This results not only from different skill levels but also from differences in the institutional and social context that shape the labor supply and employment of the two groups. Much of this contrast is rooted in the dynamics of the immigration process itself and in the transition that it involves. As native blacks can hardly recreate the conditions that characterize this process, it is unlikely that blacks could move in large numbers directly into many of the jobs vacated by immigrants even if the blacks were willing to work for low wages, as many undoubtedly are. In any case, we do know that in the past, the employment gains made by native blacks were not based in industries and jobs characterized by informal organization and employment processes, which are now disproportionately filled by immigrants.

The impact of immigration restriction on blacks would occur more indirectly. If immigrants were not available, the tighter labor market might result in growth of those sectors in which blacks are now more concentrated as competition from more immigrant-dependent sectors weakened. Thus fast-food outlets and intermediate-sector chains might increase as the number of ethnic restaurants diminished; unionized construction might have more success in the alterations and renovations sector; and inroads by nonunion contractors in large commercial projects might be reversed.

But the operation of these indirect processes would not unambiguously redound to the benefit of black men. By curtailing the supply of arriving immigrants, the immigrant-owned sectors in particular will be weakened, because both the supply of low-wage employees will decline and the markets that serve an ethnic clientele will shrink. This will release skilled and experienced immigrants previously working in those firms to compete more directly with natives.

By shrinking the population, or slowing its growth, reduced immigration would also reduce the size of public-sector employment. Therefore, immigration restrictions would possibly open jobs that have historically not benefited blacks while reducing the demand for workers in the sector of the economy that has been the foundation of black progress over the past twenty years.

But the extent of these types of adjustments, if they happen at all, and whether blacks benefit depend on a variety of market, political, and institutional factors. In the rest of this chapter I shall consider the possible changes in the industries under study and discuss evidence for the overall economy.

The Restaurant Industry

At the lower end of the restaurant industry, the fast-food and intermediate sectors would benefit from a decline in the immigrant sector. To some extent, the demand for black teenagers might grow and more blacks with postsecondary education might find work in managerial positions in the chains, but the growth of these sectors is not likely to help black adult males with low levels of educational attainment.

At the upper end of the market, black males might benefit if immigration restriction resulted in job upgrading in the full-service sector. Immigrants are employed in this sector both as unskilled and skilled (although informally trained) kitchen workers. One possible reaction would be an increase in the wages for long-term unskilled workers and for certain types of skilled workers. Although a sharp cut in immigration in the short term would set off such a wage increase, there are already observable trends in the industry that would minimize this adjustment by reducing the need for stable, long-term, and informally trained workers.

First, there will probably be a continued movement toward simplified procedures. To be sure, much of the demand for full-service meals cannot be met by the fast-food mass-production techniques. Nevertheless, the industry is developing new ways of serving and preparing higher-quality food with less-complicated cooking skills. There already has been an increase in the use of pre-prepared foods. This trend is most evident for baked goods; many high-priced restaurants now purchase rather than prepare desserts. Another possibility for maintaining quality at low prices is menu reduction. For example, one well-known New York restaurant serves only seven entrees, which allows the restaurant to serve high-quality meals at a lower price than would be otherwise possible. Under the right conditions, menu reduction could be carried further by developing chains that serve an even smaller number of high-quality products such as the recent development of chains serving crepes. Although these establishments cannot be compared to expensive French restaurants, they are serving dishes that were previously available only in full-service restaurants. Restaurateurs expect these trends to continue.

Undoubtedly, the steak house is the most important example of the use of an uncomplicated technology to serve the expensive market. Here the quality is in the food itself, not in the preparation. The cooking is simple, and most steak houses serve only a limited number of vegetables and desserts. Salaries and wages account for only 20 percent of sales in these restaurants. This is less than the wage share even in coffee shops[22] and suggests that steak houses will be a more important part of the expensive segment of the restaurant market in cities where there are few immigrants.

In addition to skill reduction in the full-service sector, immigration restriction is also likely to accelerate the current trend toward reliance on chefs and managers who have been trained in postsecondary or professional restaurant and business schools. Thus a typical restaurant will be more and more characterized by a bifurcated employment structure—formally trained managers and chefs supervising unskilled and generally short-term lower-level workers. In effect, the internal mobility opportunities in the industry are shrinking. A large supply of immigrants enhances the structure of informal training in the industry, yet the industry is already positioned to operate without that structure.

Although a contraction of the immigrant labor supply would indeed shift production away from the type of informal labor processes in which blacks have had relatively less success, the production processes that would be strengthened are not likely to increase significantly the availability of stable career-type jobs for blacks without high levels of education. Indeed, immigration restriction would probably lower the average skill level in the industry as fast-food and intermediate-sector technologies grew rather than increase the availability of skilled jobs to blacks. And any emerging better jobs not requiring formal training will not necessarily go to blacks. As we have seen, few blacks benefited from the full-service waiting jobs opened up by the reduction fifteen to twenty years ago in the supply of European-trained waiters. It is therefore not surprising that in a study using 1970 census data no statistically significant relationship was found between the proportion of black males employed in the industry in an SMSA and the percentage of the SMSA's population accounted for by the foreign born.[23] And since the 1970 data were collected, the trends that mitigate the possible benefits that blacks might enjoy as a result of immigration restriction have accelerated.

The Garment Industry

Although the labor process through which immigrants are employed in the garment industry is in many ways similar to the process in immigrant restaurants, the nature of the possible interaction and competition between foreign-born workers and native-born blacks is entirely different.

In contrast to the restaurant industry, the garment industry, like all manufacturing, differs from local industries in its vulnerability to foreign and regional competitors. And indeed employment in garment manufacturing decreased one-third between 1969 and 1975 alone—a decline largely attributable to foreign penetration of domestic markets.[24] Moreover, production has moved out of New York even faster both because of lower wages in the South, Southwest, and rural regions and because of the development of mass-production techniques that require large amounts of space and efficient access to transportation for bulk.

Due to this vulnerability to competition from other countries and regions, at least in New York, the issue of competition between immigrants and natives for garment jobs does not generate much controversy. Indeed, in contrast to much of the country's labor movement, the New York Local 23-25 of the International Ladies Garment Workers Union is opposed to restrictive immigration policies such as employer sanctions or sharp reductions in legal immigration ceilings.[25] This is hardly surprising because a significant reduction in immigration is unlikely to lead to wage increases and increased garment employment for unemployed New Yorkers; rather, it would result in further curtailment of the already shrunken employment in the city's garment industry (and, of course, an accompanying contraction in the union's membership).

Although the cheap labor made available through immigration is fundamental to the continued viability of garment production in New York, the process through which that labor is mobilized, organized, and eventually trained is particularly well suited for the manufacture of the goods that continue to be produced in the city.[26] Thus once again, the problem is not simply finding workers willing to work at low wages—even if it were desirable to maintain jobs with wages low enough to compete with firms in Hong Kong—but rather to reproduce the social system that governs this particular type of labor process.

Immigration restriction might also threaten New York's position as a fashion, design, and marketing center and the thousands of associated jobs. And it is in these related jobs, rather than in the production itself, that blacks are more likely to be found. This suggests complementarity between the two groups in this industry rather than competition.

The Construction Industry

Of the industries discussed in this book, it is in the construction industry where competition between blacks and immigrants appears to be most likely. Nevertheless, there is also an element of complementarity between the two groups in that native blacks are concentrated in the unionized sector while immigrants more often are found in open-shop firms. The competition between the groups depends on the impact that immigrants have on the growth of open-shop construction. Thus if competition from immigrant firms accelerates the relative decline of the union sector, then indirectly, black employment in the industry will be hurt by immigration.

But the growth of the open shop is a national phenomenon arising from many causes other than immigration. To the extent that immigrants are concentrated in large cities where unions tend to have strength, then competition between the groups will be blunted. Moreover, it is the nature of the construction output—residential and renovation versus commercial and institutional—as well as the strength of the unions that demarcated the sectors of black gains; thus to some extent the structural separation between the groups is independent of the open-shop growth.

In New York, the share of construction jobs going to native blacks did decline during the 1970s despite a slight increase in their share of total employment, and thus their representation fell (Table 7.1). An important cause of this drop, not revealed in comparative employment figures, was the change in the condition of the city's construction markets during the 1970s. According to Carmenza Gallo, during the 1967–1970 period, renovation and alteration accounted for only 9 percent of all construction, whereas during the 1977–1980 period, renovation accounted for more than 22 percent of total construction.[27] This pattern resulted from the collapse of commercial construction during the mid- to late 1970s. Because native blacks are more concentrated in commercial construction, this pattern helps explain the drop in black representation.

Moreover, construction employment of the foreign born also dropped relative to changes in the foreign-born population, and although nonwhite immigrants increased their share of the industry's jobs, they did so only in proportion to the increase in their share of all jobs. Indeed, it was the representation of nonblack natives that increased over the decade. Thus, although the possibility of competition

TABLE 7.1
Representation of Demographic Groups in the Construction Industry,
New York City, 1970 and 1980

| | Percentage of Employed | | Index of |
	Labor Force	Construction Workers	Representation
Black native born			
1970	14.7	12.2	83.0
1980	15.4	10.9	70.8
Native born (excluding blacks)			
1970	64.9	58.7	90.4
1980	56.7	54.1	95.4
Foreign born			
1970	20.3	29.3	144.3
1980	27.9	34.9	125.1
Foreign born (excluding whites)			
1970	7.0	5.4	77.1
1980	16.9	12.9	76.3

Source: U.S. Bureau of the Census, *Census of Population: 1970, Public Use Samples of Basic Records (5 percent Sample), New York;* and *Census of Population: 1980, Public Use Microdata Samples (Sample A), New York* (Washington, D.C.: GPO).

between the two groups remains plausible, the changing patterns of construction employment at least in New York over the 1970s do not support the argument that blacks were displaced in the industry by foreign-born workers.

The General Impact

Market, technological, and institutional factors in each of these three industries shape the competition between black men and immigrants. In the restaurant industry, emerging production technologies and increased reliance on formal training mitigate the labor market conflict between the groups; in the garment industry, it is the growth of foreign competition; and in construction, the role of the unions and government antidiscrimination enforcement. But in the end, it is the means by which the labor supplies are shaped, particularly the processes through which these groups are integrated into the labor market and acquire skills, that give scope to the factors responsible for blunting the competition between black men and immigrants.

The net effect on the overall economy will depend on the relative strength of these interactions and the interactions that take place in other industries. Despite the controversy surrounding the possible impact of immigration on native minorities, only a handful of studies have attempted to measure the impact empirically.

Thomas Muller and Thomas Espenshade used 1980 census data to compare black unemployment rates among SMSAs with varying populations of Hispanics.[28] They considered the presence of Hispanics to be a rough measure of the availability of immigrants. Although their control variables were statistically significant and had the expected signs,[29] no statistically significant relationship between the Hispanic share of the population and black unemployment was found.

One particularly interesting finding of this study concerns the possibility of internal migration away from areas of high unemployment. If blacks in particular are displaced by immigrants, they can be expected to move away from those areas with high immigrant concentration. Indeed, this reaction could disguise the impact of immigration; that is, no relationship would be found between black unemployment and immigration because displaced blacks relocate, thereby reducing unemployment. But Muller and Espenshade find that black internal migration to Southern California continued at the high level experienced during the 1960s even as Mexican immigration accelerated toward the the end of the 1970s.

George Borjas also approached this problem by analyzing the relationship between blacks and Hispanics.[30] His research was based on the 1976 *Survey of Income and Education*. Borjas derived demand equations from a production function. The dependent variable in each equation was the wage rate for each group; the independent variables were the relative presence of each group in the population of the SMSA. Borjas found that Hispanics and blacks as well as Hispanics and whites were actually complements in production. One weakness of this study for the analysis of the impact of immigration was that only 36 percent of the Hispanics were foreign born. But if Hispanics are equated with immigrants, then this result implies that black men would benefit from increased immigration of Hispanic men.

Borjas also used 1970 and 1980 census data to analyze the labor market interactions between immigrants and black men.[31] Once again, he found that the two groups were production complements rather than substitutes.

These four studies, which used three different data sets, all suggest that immigrants do not hurt the labor market position of native black men. To be sure, before a definitive measure of the interaction between the two groups can be achieved, more empirical research, using different methodologies, assumptions, and data sets is necessary. Nevertheless, it is suggestive that the results of the aggregate research are consistent with the insights of this book's case studies. Indeed, although the empirical work cited here provides evidence that the results of the case studies are not idiosyncratic, the case studies themselves provide a more concrete understanding of statistical results that, given common assumptions about the roles and interactions of these groups, at first appear counterintuitive.

Notes

1. Harvard Sitkoff, *A New Deal for Blacks: The Emergence of Civil Rights as a National Issue* (New York, N.Y.: Oxford University Press, 1978).

2. Michael Hout, "Occupational Mobility of Black Men: 1962 to 1973," *American Sociological Review* 49 (1984): 316.

3. Richard B. Freeman, "Troubled Workers in the Labor Market," Discussion Paper No. 881 (Cambridge, Mass.: Harvard Institute of Economic Research, February, 1982).

4. Marshall I. Pomer, "Labor Market Structure, Intragenerational Mobility, and Discrimination: Black Male Advancement out of Low-Paying Occupations, 1962–1973," *American Sociological Review* 51 (October 1986): 650–659.

5. U.S. Bureau of the Census, *Census of Population: 1980, Public Use Microdata Samples (Sample A), New York* (Washington, D.C.: GPO).

6. Freeman, 1982, p. 36.

7. Jonathan Leonard, "The Effect of Unions on the Employment of Blacks, Hispanics, and Women," *Industrial and Labor Relations Review* 39 (October 1985): 115–132.

8. U.S. Bureau of the Census, *Census of Population: 1980, Public Use Microdata Samples.*

9. Black organizations currently trying to open construction jobs for blacks concentrate entirely on unionized construction sites rather than establishing black firms or opening opportunities in the nonunion sector. Members of these organizations argue that they have been unfairly barred from the more desirable unionized jobs and should therefore devote their efforts to breaking down those barriers. Turning to the nonunion or renovation sectors would represent a capitulation to union and contractor discrimination. Interview by Carmenza Gallo with members of "Fight Back."

10. Several articles analyzing the impact of equal opportunity enforcement in the late 1960s and early 1970s appear in the July 1976 issue of *Industrial and Labor Relations Review.*

11. Jonathan Leonard, "What Promises are Worth: The Impact of Affirmative Action Goals," *Journal of Human Resources* 20 (Winter 1985): 3–20; Jonathan Leonard, "Antidiscrimination or Reverse Discrimination: The

Impact of Changing Demographics, Title VII, and Affirmative Action on Productivity," *Journal of Human Resources* 19 (Spring 1984): 145–174; and Jonathan Leonard, "The Impact of Affirmative Action on Employment," *Journal of Labor Economics* 2 (October 1984): 439–463.

12. Thierry J. Noyelle, *Beyond Industrial Dualism: Market and Job Segmentation in the New Economy* (Boulder Colo.: Westview Press, 1987) , chapter 2.

13. Herbert R. Northrup and John A. Larson, *The Impact of the AT&T-EEO Consent Decree,* Labor Relations and Public Policy Series, the Wharton School, University of Pennsylvania, 20 (1979); and Casey C. Ichniowski, "Have Angels Done More? The Steel Industry Consent Decree," *Industrial and Labor Relations Review* 36 (January 1983): 182–198.

14. Noyelle, 1987, chapter 2.

15. Carol Stack, *All Our Kin* (New York, N.Y.: Harper and Row, 1974).

16. Paul Osterman, *Getting Started: The Youth Labor Market* (Cambridge, Mass.: MIT Press, 1980), p. 144.

17. Ivan Charner and Bryna Shore Fraser, *Fast Food Jobs* (Washington, D.C.: National Institute for Work and Learning, 1984), p. 15.

18. Henry Jay Becher, "Personal Networks of Opportunity in Obtaining Jobs: Racial Differences and Effects of Segregation," Report No. 281 (Baltimore, Md.: Center for Social Organization of Schools, Johns Hopkins University, August 1979), table 1.

19. Barbara Bergmann and William Darity argue that blacks often have limited access to managerial jobs because white owners and managers believe that blacks can interact more efficiently with supervisory personnel who share their cultural and ethnic background and that white subordinates will resist supervision by blacks. This is not a problem for immigrants in ethnic restaurants. Barbara R. Bergmann and William Darity, Jr., "Social Relations in the Workplace and Employer Discrimination," Industrial Relations Research Association Series, Proceedings of the Thirty-third Annual Meeting, 1980: 155–162.

20. This argument helps explain why federal efforts to promote black self-employment, primarily by providing loans, have been frustrating. Financial capital is only one requirement for successful entrepreneurship. Unless public policy can act on some of the other barriers faced by black entrepreneurs, a financial assistance strategy is unlikely to work. This suggests that contract set-asides for black construction firms linked to financial assistance might be more successful because the unions could provide the trained work force. Thus the role of networks in finding clients and in recruiting and training a work force is reduced. Indeed, Carmenza Gallo found that set-asides and government contracts in general were important for the development of many of the black-owned firms in her sample. Carmenza Gallo, "The Construction Industry in New York City: Immigrants and Black Entrepreneurs," Working Paper (New York, N.Y.: Conservation of Human Resources, Columbia University, 1983).

21. A 1968 comparison of black and white businessmen found that white entrepreneurs tended to acquire their entrepreneurial skills through personal

relationships, but blacks were more dependent on formal institutions. David Caplowitz, "A Profile of Black and White Businessmen," in David Caplowitz, ed., *The Merchants of Harlem: A Study of Small Business in a Black Community* (Beverly Hills, Cal.: Sage Publications, 1973).

22. Daryl D. Wyckoff and W. Earl Sasser, *The Chain-Restaurant Industry* (Lexington, Mass.: Lexington Books, 1978), p. xlviii.

23. The dependent variable for this regression was the ratio of black male employment in the restaurant industry to the total black labor force. The independent variables included the proportion of the SMSA population accounted for by the foreign born, whether the SMSA was in the South, the total population and per capita income of the SMSA, the percentage of SMSA employment accounted for by durable manufacturing, and the black male share of total population. Although the coefficient for the foreign-born variable was negative, it was less than one-third the magnitude of its standard error. For a detailed discussion, see Thomas Bailey, "Labor Market Competition and Economic Mobility in Low Wage Employment: A Case Study of Immigrants in the Restaurant Industry" (PhD dissertation, Economics Department, Massachusetts Institute of Technology, 1983), chapter 7.

24. Roger Waldinger, *Through the Eye of the Needle: Immigrant Enterprise in New York's Garment Trades* (New York, N.Y.: New York University Press, 1986), chapter 3.

25. Muzaffar Chisti, "Immigration Policy Examined," *Dollars and Sense*, June 1985: 13.

26. Waldinger, 1986, chapter 4.

27. Gallo, 1983, table 1.

28. Thomas Muller and Thomas Espenshade, *The Fourth Wave: California's Newest Immigrants* (Washington, D.C.: The Urban Institute, 1985), p. 101.

29. The controls used were the rate of population growth, the percentage of income earned in construction and durable goods manufacturing, the percentage of blacks twenty-five years and older with at least a high school education, and the rate of unemployment for whites.

30. George Borjas, "The Substitutability of Blacks, Hispanics and White Labor," *Economic Inquiry* 21 (1983): 93–106.

31. George Borjas, "The Demographic Determinants of the Demand for Black Labor," in Richard B. Freeman and Harry J. Holzer, eds., *The Black Youth Employment Crisis* (Chicago, Ill.: University of Chicago Press, 1986), pp. 191–230; and George Borjas, "Immigrants, Minorities, and Labor Market Competition," *Industrial and Labor Relations Review* 40 (April 1987): 382–392.

8

The Impact of Legal Status

For many years, undocumented immigration has been the focus of the policy debate. This book has taken a broader view, concentrating on the impact of immigration in general. Indeed, the factors emphasized here that differentiate immigrants from otherwise similar workers—for example, the transition between economies and cultures, the importance of networks—apply to both legal resident aliens and undocumented workers. But many researchers, journalists, and politicians argue that legal status is fundamental in shaping the labor market role of the undocumented.[1] In this chapter I argue that on the contrary, a consideration of legal status will not alter the analysis developed in this book in any important way.

Discussion of undocumented employment is complicated theoretically because at least three conceptually distinct factors contribute to the labor market impact of undocumented workers. First, illegal immigration increases the total number of immigrants. Second, to the extent that undocumented aliens possess labor market characteristics different from those of other immigrants, their presence will change the overall distribution of demographic characteristics within the population for any given level of total immigration.[2] And finally, legal status itself may influence the labor market effect of immigration because undocumented immigrants are legally vulnerable, they may be willing to accept jobs at lower wages than they would if they had a legal right to work, or they may be subject to intimidation by employers.

Most discussions of the impact of illegal immigrants fail to differentiate among these three factors.[3] Yet, recent changes in immigration policy and other proposals that may be implemented in the future will influence these three factors differentially. For example, the amnesty program will emend legal status and the temporary-worker program will alter the distribution of the demographic characteristics of immigrants without necessarily causing the other changes that would be expected from decreases or increases in the total number of illegals.

In this chapter I shall focus on the third factor: the independent effect of legal status. The question here is what the effect would be of legalizing the status of all undocumented workers without changing the total number of immigrants or the distribution of demographic characteristics among them. This is a particularly topical issue because it addresses the short-term labor market impacts of an amnesty program, although the amnesty provision of the 1986 immigration law would not bring about complete regularization of all undocumented workers.

In contrast to the conclusions cited above, the argument in this book is that the legal status of immigrants has only a secondary influence on the labor market: Replacement of all illegals with resident aliens who are otherwise similar would affect the labor market only minimally. Available evidence from surveys and industry case studies is consistent with this hypothesis, although data limitations preclude definite confirmation. This conclusion implies that amnesty for the undocumented will not have a major, long-term labor market impact although it will undoubtedly improve the lives of eligible illegal residents.[4]

Additional purposes of this chapter are to clarify the discussion and analysis of the impact of legal status, to highlight the important factors that determine the employment impact of illegal residents, and to discuss systematically how legal status interacts with the labor market. Despite the widespread concern about illegal immigration, the effect of illegality per se has never been analyzed systematically, even at a theoretical level. One conclusion is that particular changes in the institutional regulation of the labor market have important influences on the labor market impact of legal status.

This chapter first addresses the influence of legal status on market wage levels and considers the effects on minimum-wage enforcement and the level of unionization. Following that discussion, employer awareness of legal status is addressed.

Market Wages

The simplest labor market model suggests that an increase in the supply of labor will result in a drop in the wage level, at least in the short run. Although in the formal model this results from the negative relationship between the demand for labor and the wage level, for the general public it seems plausible that if employers can choose from a larger pool of workers, employers can offer lower wages. However, under consideration in this chapter is a change only in legal status without an increase in the number of workers. In this case, if wages did fall, the decrease would not result from an increase in the size of the potential labor supply but rather from an increase in the number of hours each immigrant is available to work at a given wage level. For example, if illegals had a lower reservation wage, then there would be wage levels that legals might reject but at which illegals would be willing to work. This might happen if employers intimidated undocumented workers into accepting lower wages, if the undocumented limited their job search because of fear or desire to remain inconspicuous, or if the undocumented were more inclined to accept low-wage jobs because they lacked access to unemployment insurance or other income support programs. In these cases, an amnesty program would result in higher wages to the extent that workers would no longer fear their legal vulnerability.

In developing empirical tests for the labor market effects of legal status, it is useful to separate two issues. The first issue is whether there are wage gaps between otherwise similar legal and illegal immigrants; the second issue is whether the unique characteristics of illegals, and perhaps their lower reservation wages, reduce wages for the workers with whom they compete. Each issue is addressed below.

Wage Differentials

In a recent newspaper article, a reporter, after talking to several immigration experts, concluded that "it is generally accepted that illegal aliens have to work more for less."[5] Such an earnings gap would be strong evidence that the treatment of illegals in the labor market is different from the treatment of legals. It would suggest that legal status does indeed have an effect.

The wage-gap hypothesis is widely accepted, but a closer look suggests that the conceptual basis of the argument is weak. Although legal vulnerability undoubtedly influences the search for employment and the willingness to bargain for higher wages, the strength of this effect depends largely on the information available to the immigrant. An illegal alien who is isolated and has contact with only one or two employers is more likely to end up in a job with unusually low wages than one who is integrated into a network of family and friends with experience and contacts in the labor market. Networks are particularly strong among the undocumented—immigrants who have family and contacts in the United States are more likely to be able to work illegally than their unconnected counterparts. Additionally, the legal system that regulates immigration favors aliens with families already in the United States.

In large urban areas, both legal and undocumented recent immigrants are usually integrated into well-established immigrant communities. They find work with small firms, many of which are owned by immigrants or are located in immigrant neighborhoods. The undocumented will therefore have many sources of information about their labor market prospects.

Legal status is more likely to influence wage levels in areas and occupations where illegals are isolated and where immigrants are less likely to have information about other jobs or the means to get to them. But the effects of isolation on southwestern ranches highlight the differences in the labor market that result from the more plentiful information in urban areas. This is illustrated in the following statement by a rancher near San Diego:

> There is an invisible fence about five miles from here (the Orange County line). Once our man crosses that fence and decides to venture into the whole different world of Anaheim, Santa Ana and L.A., and he lives there, say six months, when he comes back he would be a total misfit. The term is: he has adopted the Gringo way. He has also been exposed to things he has never heard of such as fringe benefits, unionism, etc.[6]

This rancher's employment strategy depends on having an adequate supply of workers who have not yet crossed the "invisible line." But in large urban areas, immigrants are immediately exposed to these aspects of the labor market. Hence, newcomers would rapidly become "misfits" in this sense.

Therefore, on conceptual or theoretical grounds, there are reasons to question the argument that illegals are paid less than legals for the same work. Moreover, as we shall see below, empirical support for the argument is also weak.

General Wage Depression

Although a wage gap for legals and illegals with similar characteristics would be evidence that legal status does influence the labor market, the absence of such a wage gap does not necessarily imply that legal status has no influence. It is possible that if illegals had different labor supply characteristics or lower reservation wages due to their legal status, their labor market availability would reduce wages for all groups of workers with whom they compete.

Restricted access to unemployment insurance and other income support programs is potentially an influential factor in distinguishing the labor supply functions of otherwise similar legal and illegal aliens. There is an ongoing controversy in the literature concerning the use of unemployment benefits and income transfers by the undocumented.[7] Nevertheless, it is likely that illegals have more restricted access to nonlabor market sources of income than otherwise similar legals, although the availability of assistance from family and community networks and the possibility of returning to the home country suggest that dependence of illegal residents for subsistence on the labor market is less than absolute.

Although data are available to carry out rough tests of the wage-gap hypothesis, testing of the general wage-depression hypothesis is not currently possible. Therefore, we are left with the conclusions implied by the analysis of the wage gap between the two groups of aliens. Depending on which model of the underlying labor market is used, some inferences still can be drawn from the absence of a disparity between the wages of otherwise similar legals and illegals.

In a perfectly competitive market model, the wages for similar workers will equalize; therefore, the absence of a wage gap is still consistent with a negative effect of legal status. But if the labor market is divided or segmented in the sense that low-wage employers in some segments—the open sector—find it easier to hire illegals than employers in other segments—the closed sector—then differences in the reservation wages or the labor supply functions among the two groups could still be reflected in a wage gap. In this case, illegals would obviously be concentrated in the open sector. Assuming that the presence of illegals results in a lower wage in that sector, documented workers would tend to seek work in the closed sector where wages would be higher. In this case, as long as the open sector were not too large relative to the closed sector, then equally productive legals and illegals would receive different wages. Thus, although this argument cannot be considered definitive, given the imperfections and institutions that influence the labor market, it seems likely that major differences in treatment between legals and illegals would also be reflected in differences between the wages received by the two groups.

Empirical Tests of Wage Disparity

Although the newspaper article referred to earlier concluded that "illegals work for less," no supporting study was cited. Indeed, according to the article, a study by Glauco Peres of Dominicans in New York concluded that "there was almost no difference in job experience or income levels of aliens based on legal status."[8] Peres compared the first-job earnings and characteristics of illegals with those in his sample with a legal right to work and concluded that there are no important differences in wage levels and occupations between the two groups.[9]

To be sure, average wages for other samples of undocumented aliens are invariably low—$2.71 per hour in a sample of apprehended illegals interviewed by David North and Marion Houstoun in 1975;[10] $3.01 per hour for illegal male restaurant workers and $2.93 for illegal male garment workers in a sample of Hispanics collected in California in 1979; and in her study of Dominicans in New York, Sherri Grasmuck found that over 40 percent of illegal Dominican men earned less than $150 a week in 1981.[11] Although these wages are low, low wages and indeed pay in violation of minimum-wage laws are not limited to undocumented workers. Thus, the issue is whether the wages received by illegals are low when compared to wages of other immigrants who resemble illegals. The North-Houstoun sample has no comparison group of legals. Grasmuck found lower wages among illegals even though "type of job and industrial sector did not differ significantly for documented and undocumented immigrants."[12] Grasmuck also found that, on average, illegals achieved higher educational levels in their home country than legals, but she also suggested that the illegals had been in the United States for less time than their legal counterparts. Among Sheldon Maram's respondents, 4 percent of whom were born in the United States, although the citizen and legal resident Hispanics tended to earn more than the illegals—an average of $4.21 and $3.01 in restaurants and the garment industry respectively—the legals, on average, had more education, were older, had been in the United States more time, and had worked longer for their current employers. All of these differences have been shown to be associated with higher earnings.

But how much of the wage gap can be accounted for by these differences? To calculate this, estimates of the relationship between demographic characteristics and earnings are needed. Barry Chiswick has estimated earnings functions for many samples of foreign-born workers including samples from the 1970 census and the North-Houstoun sample of apprehended illegals.[13] The coefficients from his regressions are estimates of the percentage change in wages associated with a unit change in the value of each variable and can be used to ask how much the hourly wages of the average undocumented male restaurant worker would rise if he had the same education, age, and time since immigration as the average legal Hispanic restaurant worker. According to this exercise, the differences in demographic characteristics account for 80 percent of the wage gap.[14] Moreover, the gap between the average wages for the female permanent residents and illegal female restaurant workers is only 11 percent, although the differences in schooling, age, and years since immigration between these two groups of women are similar to those for the men.

Chiswick's estimates based on the 1970 census for all foreign born can be used to ask how much the wages of legal male restaurant workers would fall if they had the same characteristics as the undocumented restaurant workers. In this case, the differences in the demographic characteristics more than account for the wage gap.[15]

The purpose of these calculations is not to arrive at a precise estimate of the relationship between the earnings of legals and illegals, adjusted for background characteristics. And applying coefficient estimates to a population different from the population on which the estimates are based can be unreliable. More and better comparable data on the undocumented and on those immigrants with a legal right to work are needed for reliable measurements. Despite these problems, it does appear that at least a large part of the gap between the wages of legal and illegal Hispanics can be explained by the differences in their characteristics when estimates of the influence of those characteristics are applied to the data.

Enforcement of the Minimum Wage

The previous section addressed the effect of legal status per se on the market wage. But in many immigrant-employing industries, the legislated minimum is above the market wage. If there is full compliance with the minimum wage in these industries, then the wage level is set by the legislature, and the legal status of the work force has no influence on the wage level. Therefore, to the extent that legality influences the wage level in the presence of a minimum wage, it must do so through its effect on compliance. Legal status might affect compliance if the presence of many undocumented workers were to thwart enforcement.

In this section, the effect of legal status on minimum-wage compliance is analyzed using a simple model developed by Orley Ashenfelter and Robert Smith.[16] They argue that employers will weigh the wage savings from noncompliance against the penalty for violation, adjusted for the probability of getting caught. If the penalty is held constant, compliance will be low when the probability of detection is low and when the difference between the market wage and the minimum wage is high. Assuming, as was argued above, that the relative number of permanent resident and undocumented aliens of equal productivity has only a weak influence on the underlying wage rate, the influence of legal status must operate primarily through the probability of detection.

Illegals and Noncompliance

Surveys indeed find that many illegals are paid subminimum wages.[17] But the question to be addressed here is whether employers can avoid compliance with minimum-wage laws *because* of the presence of undocumented workers. Given the number of firms that might have an incentive to violate the law and the resources available for enforcement, it is not surprising that noncompliance is widespread; but this balance of benefits and potential costs does not necessarily depend on the immigration status of the labor supply.

In the past, a frequent argument was that employers of the undocumented could violate minimum-wage laws with impunity because they could threaten to report workers to the immigration authorities if workers object to their treatment.[18] According to the compliance model, the probability of getting caught is therefore low. But under the 1986 immigration law, it is a crime to hire an illegal. Reporting troublesome undocumented workers to the authorities will therefore be self-incrimination. And even before the reform, the use of this tactic was not without disadvantages to the employer. Turning in workers increased the chances that the employer's minimum-wage violations would be discovered. Thus, employing the undocumented may have lowered the probability of getting caught, but reporting undocumented workers raised it again. The new law only adds to the dangers of this strategy.

The reluctance of the undocumented to report violations of the law is a more serious threat to minimum-wage enforcement. This is particularly important since in many states the enforcement system is based on complaint investigation. To the extent that illegals do not report violations, the probability of getting caught will be lower for employers who hire many illegals.

But conversely, one implication of the compliance model is that incentives to violate the minimum-wage law will not be influenced by the legal status of the work force if the enforcement system is based on random inspection. It could be argued that such a system might not reveal so many violations, but it would eliminate the difference in incentives attributable to legal status. Therefore, the argument in support of the virtually unchallenged assumption that the undocumented thwart minimum-wage enforcement is based on the use of complaint-based enforcement, a procedure that the California enforcement authority has found to be ineffective in finding "the overwhelming majority of violations."[19]

Empirical Evidence

The above argument suggests that controlling for the underlying market wage rate, subminimum wages should not be more widespread for illegals than for other workers so long as the enforcement system is not complaint based. Data on wages of illegal and legal Hispanic immigrants in the garment and restaurant industries collected by Maram in California can be used to analyze this hypothesis because the enforcement system in these industries "sought inclusivity" and therefore did not depend on complaint-based investigation.[20]

In this book, the Ashenfelter and Smith measure of compliance is used in order to facilitate comparison with their results. Ashenfelter and Smith use a simple measure that is the ratio of all workers earning exactly the minimum to the sum of those workers and all workers earning less than the minimum. They assume that if there were full compliance, all workers who would have earned below the minimum would be paid exactly the minimum. Ashenfelter and Smith present an extensive discussion of the possible biases in this measure but conclude that they do not amount to fundamental problems.

Using data from the 1975 *Civilian Population Surveys*, they calculate a compliance ratio of .60. They conclude that "while substantial, compliance with the minimum wage law is anything but complete."[21]

Maram's data were collected in 1979, but the real value of the minimum wage and the ratio of the minimum to the manufacturing wage in 1975 were close to their values in 1979. Therefore, it is appropriate to compare Maram's 1979 data with Ashenfelter and Smith's data for 1975.

Table 8.1 presents the distribution of wage rates from the Maram sample for Hispanic workers in the garment and restaurant industries and the compliance ratios. The ratio for the restaurant industry is above the ratio for 1975 calculated by Ashenfelter and Smith. For the garment industry, it is much lower (.47), although the piece rates that prevail in the industry complicate enforcement. Compliance for illegals is lower than for legals.

Higher compliance for legal residents and U.S. citizens suggests that the lower probability of detection creates a greater incentive for employers not to comply for the undocumented. But this does not take account of possible differences in the underlying market wages. Employers have a greater incentive to violate the law for those workers whose market wage is farthest below the minimum.[22] Therefore, compliance ratios should be lowest for the groups for which the distribution of underlying market wages is weighted more heavily toward those wages farthest below the minimum.

TABLE 8.1
Wage Rates and Compliance Ratios for Hispanic Restaurant and Garment Workers, Los Angeles County, 1979

| | Garment Workers | | | | | | | | |
| | Total | | | Hispanic Undocumented | | | U.S. Citizen/Permanent Resident Alien | | |
Wage	Total	Male	Female	Total	Male	Female	Total	Male	Female
Percent Receiving:									
$2.00 or less	18.0	15.1	18.9	19.9	16.5	21.2	4.9	—	6.1
$2.01–$2.89	17.3	17.6	17.3	19.3	19.4	19.1	9.7	6.7	10.6
$2.90	32.1	33.7	31.5	33.9	36.9	32.8	22.0	13.3	22.7
$2.91 or more	32.6	33.6	32.3	26.9	27.2	26.9	63.4	80.0	60.8
Compliance ratio	.47	.50	.46	.46	.50	.44	.60	.66	.57
Sample size[a]	499	123	375	403	105	298	84	16	67
	Restaurant Workers								
Percent Receiving:									
$2.00 or less	6.9	6.3	9.4	8.4	7.7	12.2	2.8	2.0	4.3
$2.01–$2.89	11.4	9.9	17.2	13.4	11.7	22.0	5.6	4.1	8.7
$2.90	40.7	39.3	45.2	42.4	41.8	43.8	29.2	20.4	47.9
$2.91 or more	41.0	44.5	28.2	35.8	38.8	22.0	62.4	73.5	39.1
Compliance ratio	.68	.74	.62	.66	.68	.56	.83	.76	.78
Sample size	327	258	67	244	200	42	76	51	25

[a]Sex was not reported for three observations so the numbers of males and females do not always add up to the totals.

Source: Sheldon L. Maram, *Hispanic Workers in the Garment and Restaurant Industries in Los Angeles County: A Social and Economic Profile* (Fullerton, Cal.: California State University and Department of Industrial Relations of the State of California, 1980), pp. 32, 92.

Maram's data do suggest that within each industry, the underlying wages are indeed lower for illegals than for legal residents.[23] Although it cannot be concluded from these data that the legal status of the workers in the sample did not affect compliance through thwarting enforcement, the pattern of compliance can be explained using the compliance model without assuming that illegality hampers enforcement. Finally, judging from Ashenfelter and Smith's results and after accounting for the pattern of underlying market wages and the problem of labor standards administration in the presence of piece rates, compliance in the restaurant and garment industries (both of which employ many undocumented workers) is not much different from compliance in the country as a whole. This is consistent with the hypothesis of this chapter that legality per se will have little effect on compliance so long as enforcement procedures are not complaint based.

Complaint-Based Enforcement

But what about a complaint-based system? As argued above, in such a system it appears that noncompliant employers will have a lower chance of being caught if they employ undocumented workers. Nevertheless, although many states rely primarily on complaint investigation, analysis of enforcement patterns does indicate that in most cases, some resources are concentrated in those areas where violations are most likely.[24] For example, more resources are devoted to enforcement in the South where lower prevailing wages create greater incentives for noncompliance. Therefore, although scattered violations are harder to detect if illegals are afraid to complain, widespread noncompliance in an industry or area, by attracting the general attention of the enforcement authorities, will result in a movement away from complaint-based enforcement and a reduction in the influence of legality on the incentives to comply.

In the end, whether or not the presence of illegal immigrants undermines the enforcement of the minimum wage is rapidly becoming unimportant. It should be emphasized that enforcement of the Fair Labor Standards Act is already lax. Although the responsibilities of the federal enforcement agencies have grown over the past fifteen years, their resources have not. Furthermore, the federal minimum wage has not increased since 1981, and unless it is raised in the near future, as prices and market wages rise, the federal legal wage floor will become increasingly irrelevant.

Unionization

The legal vulnerability of undocumented workers is often cited as a significant barrier to unionization in the industries in which they account for a large percentage of the labor force.[25] Surprisingly, surveys of undocumented aliens disclose considerable union membership. About 16 percent of the undocumented illegals interviewed by David North and Marion Houstoun in 1975 were union members. Among nonagricultural workers in the sample, 20 percent belonged to unions.[26] If the pattern of employment among industries had been the same as that in the North-Houstoun sample, then approximately 23 percent of all workers and 28 percent of production workers would have been unionized.[27]

The probability of union membership in the North-Houstoun sample rose with the length of time that the immigrant has been in the United States. Twenty-six percent of those who had been in the country for more than two years were union members, whereas the figure for more recent arrivals was only 5 percent. Thirty-seven and 24 percent of the aliens in the sample who worked in New York and Los Angeles, respectively, were union members; according to the Freeman and Medoff estimates, the figures for the two cities were 32 and 23 percent for all workers, and 50 and 35 percent for production workers.

In Maram's sample, only 4 percent of the illegal restaurant workers and 17 percent of the legals were unionized, compared to 8 percent for the industry nationally. Restaurants are usually organized along craft lines, and the difference between the legals and the illegals in Maram's sample may be due to different occupational distributions for the two groups.

The evidence from these surveys suggests that illegals have a rate of unionization that is slightly below unionization levels for the relevant industries and cities, although it is possible that much of the difference would disappear if the appropriate variables were controlled. In this respect, the rise in unionization with the length of stay in the United States is most suggestive. Sherri Grasmuck, however, found much lower unionization rates among undocumented Dominicans when compared to legal residents.[28]

The threat that illegals pose to unionization is usually believed to be in their reluctance to participate in union organizing efforts. In this type of situation, employers are most likely to use direct threats of exposure to the INS, although under the employer-sanctions provision of the 1986 immigration law, this strategy will be less attractive to employers. Overall unionization rates do not provide much information about the effects on organizing efforts because those rates may include undocumented immigrants who find jobs in firms that are already unionized and who join automatically when hired. In Grasmuck's sample, legal immigrants more often than illegals worked in firms where some kind of workplace struggle had occurred. And there is anecdotal evidence that intimidation and threats are used in these circumstances. Nevertheless, other anecdotes indicate that not all of the undocumented avoid involvement in organizing efforts.[29]

Furthermore, emphasis on the problems associated with organizing illegals has obscured other reasons why immigrants are difficult to organize. First, to the extent that immigrants view their stays as temporary, they have little commitment to their jobs. Second, those immigrants who are aspiring entrepreneurs are not likely to favor unionization of what they see as their future work force. Finally, the immigrant-owned businesses that employ many of the foreign born are often characterized by complex employment relationships that thwart the efforts of union organizers. For example, of the approximately 2,000 Chinese restaurants in New York City, only about ten are organized, even though the city's Chinese undocumented population is relatively small.

Many illegals work in industries that are extremely difficult to organize under any circumstances. The restaurant industry is a good example. In fact, the industry is probably becoming increasingly more difficult to organize, primarily because of the large proportion of teenagers and part-time females who comprise the industry's typical work force. In New York, even restaurant owners who rely on full-time workers expect their young, middle-class waiters and waitresses to be as resistant to unionization as their undocumented workers. Both legal and illegal flows of newcomers provide stable long-term workers to industries that would otherwise rely on workers with weaker labor force attachment. Workers who are committed to the labor force and the industry are much more likely to see unionization as in their interests than transient, part-time workers. For these reasons, there is no simple relationship between the presence of undocumented workers and the strength of unions in low-wage industries. There are restaurant unions in New York, Los Angeles, and San Francisco despite the presence of many illegals in those cities, but there are no restaurant unions in most southern cities, although there are fewer immigrant workers, legal or illegal, in the region.

Employer Knowledge of Legal Status

Although many native-born employers in low-wage industries in areas with large immigrant populations are aware that some or many of their workers might be undocumented, surveys conducted before the enactment of the 1986 immigration reform suggested that employers did not know the immigration status of particular individuals. In the previously cited North-Houstoun sample, 38.8 percent of the illegals believed their employers knew that they were undocumented, but 80 percent of this group were "Mexicans who were working, with very few exceptions, in the Southwest or, to a lesser extent, in California."[30] A case study conducted in San Diego by Community Research Associates concluded that employers usually took a "see-no-evil" attitude about the immigration status of their Mexican workers.[31] And 45 percent of a sample of restaurant workers in California had not been required to provide any identification to get their jobs; another 46 percent only presented a social security card.[32] Interviews conducted in the construction, nursing home, and home health care industries in New York suggest that documentation required for employment in these industries was not adequate to determine immigration status.[33]

These studies suggest that most firms used hiring practices that did not bar illegals, but that also did not seek them out. Although employers are aware that there is a good chance that they hire undocumented aliens, they do not know the immigration status of a particular worker. Under the 1986 immigration law, employers are more likely to require documents. Therefore, those illegals who they hire will probably have false documents and employers will know even less about the status of their workers. Of course, employer ignorance of legal status is not necessarily evidence that legality per se has no influence, but that whatever influence it does have operates more through broader impersonal forces than through direct intimidation of individual employees by the managers and owners of the establishments in which they work.

Conclusions

In this chapter I analyze the independent influence of legal status on the labor market effects of immigration. The conceptual experiment carried out considers the labor market changes that would take place if all undocumented workers were replaced by otherwise similar legal resident aliens.

If illegal residents have access to information about the local labor market and if they are integrated into immigrant networks and communities, legal status will have little effect on the market wage, in the absence of institutional influences on the wage rate such as the minimum wage, unionism, and access to unemployment insurance. When the minimum wage is above the market wage, the presence of illegal aliens will thwart enforcement of the minimum *if* enforcement is complaint based. Because the industries employing illegal aliens are for the most part industries with records of labor standards violations, enforcement resources that are not complaint based are likely already to be directed to those industries. Where there is little enforcement of any kind, the effect of the presence of undocumented workers on enforcement is irrelevant.

The rate of unionization among illegals is determined primarily by the rate of unionization in the industries in which they find work. Legal status is most likely to have an effect on union organizing; there is anecdotal evidence that threats of exposure to the INS are used to discourage participation in organizing activities, but even when no immigrants are available, unions currently face formidable obstacles in organizing in all industries. Thus, there is no simple relationship between union strength and the presence of undocumented aliens in a particular city.

This book emphasizes the transitional nature of the immigration process and the expectations, opportunities, social resources, and limitations that result from that process as the distinguishing causes of the immigrant labor market role. A primary objective of this chapter has been to determine whether legal status is also a fundamental determinant of the unique role of immigrants. Although the lack of relevant data will always thwart a definitive analysis of this issue, the data that are available suggest that legal status is of only secondary importance in shaping the employment and impact of immigrants.

Notes

1. David North and Allen Le Bel, *Manpower Immigration Policies in the United States*, Special Report No. 20 (Washington, D.C.: National Commission for Manpower Policy, 1978); Alejandro Portes, "Labor Functions of Illegal Aliens," *Society* 14 (September/October 1977): 31–37; and Saskia Sassen-Koob, "Immigrant and Minority Workers in the Organization of the Labor Process," *Journal of Ethnic Studies* 8 (Spring 1982): 181–212.

2. For example, undocumented workers on average may have lower skill or educational levels than immigrants who arrive initially as permanent resident aliens. If this is true, then even if the undocumented flow were numerically replaced by legal immigration, the overall impact would change because the higher-skilled newcomers would seek different jobs and compete with different groups of native-born workers.

3. In addition, the prevalence of status regularization blurs the distinction between resident and undocumented aliens. For example, in a study of Dominican residents in New York, Glauco Peres found that of the 291 resident aliens or citizens in his sample, ninety-four (about one-third) had worked

illegally and subsequently adjusted their status. Of these, sixty-one had adjusted their status in five or fewer years. Glauco Peres, "Dominican Illegals in New York: Selected Preliminary Findings," Working Paper (New York, N.Y.: New York University, Center for Latin American Studies, May 1981), figures 1 and 2. The ratio of total resident aliens admitted to resident aliens admitted through status adjustment is another indication of this phenomenon. In fiscal years 1980 and 1981, approximately 36 percent of all admitted resident aliens were admitted through status adjustment. U.S. Department of Justice, Immigration and Naturalization Service, *1980 Statistical Yearbook of the Immigration and Naturalization Service* (Washington, D.C.: GPO, 1980), and *1981 Statistical Yearbook of the Immigration and Naturalization Service* (Washington, D.C.: GPO, 1981). Through this process, past illegal flows have had an effect on the present population of legal immigrants. Estimates of the effect of removing all current illegals from the labor market could not be used to predict the ramifications of strict enforcement because the estimates would not account for the effects of previous illegal immigration on the present legal population.

4. This book is concerned primarily with immigrants who live in urban areas. Thus the argument may not apply to undocumented immigrants working in agricultural or isolated rural areas. Although agriculture is an important employer of the undocumented, employment of illegal aliens is increasingly an urban phenomenon.

5. Elaine Sciolino, "Illegal Aliens: Impact in City is Uncertain," *New York Times*, September 17, 1984, p. 1.

6. Community Research Associates, *The Employer's View: Implications for a Guestworker Program* (San Diego, Cal.: Community Research Associates, 1981).

7. A recent study by Weintraub found little use of welfare, food stamps, and unemployment insurance among a sample of illegals in Texas. Sidney Weintraub, "Illegal Immigrants in Texas: Impact on Social Services and Related Considerations," *International Migration Review* 18 (Fall 1984): 733–747. These findings are consistent with the results of a study which found use of these programs by individuals in the study to be rare. David North and Marion F. Houstoun, *The Characteristics and Role of Illegal Aliens in the U.S. Labor Market: An Exploratory Study* (Washington, D.C.: Linton, 1976), pp. 145, 148. Nevertheless, North later argued that these rates were low, at least partly as a result of the characteristics of the illegals in their sample—predominantly healthy young males who would have low rates of utilization of these programs under any circumstances. North goes on to cite a study by Van Arsdol that showed significant welfare use by illegals. Another study by North also found substantial use of employment insurance by the undocumented in California. In a sample of 147 aliens who had been apprehended and who had worked between 1975 and 1980 in a job covered by unemployment insurance, 35 percent had collected unemployment insurance benefits during this period. North concluded that "illegal receipt of income transfer payments may be much more substantial than survey data indicate." David North, "Impact of Legal, Illegal, and Refugee Migration on the U.S. Social Service Programs," in

Mary M. Kritz (ed., *U.S. Immigration and Refugee Policy: Global and Domestic Issues* (Lexington, Mass.: Lexington Books, 1983), pp. 278, 279; and M. D. Van Arsdol et al., *Non-apprehended and Apprehended Undocumented Residents in the Los Angeles Labor Market: An Exploratory Study* (Los Angeles, Cal.: University of Southern California Press, 1979).

8. Sciolino, 1984, p. B7.

9. Peres, 1981.

10. North and Houstoun, 1976, p. 116.

11. Sheldon L. Maram, *Hispanic Workers in the Garment and Restaurant Industries in Los Angeles County: A Social and Economic Profile* (Fullerton, Cal.: California State University and Department of Industrial Relations of the State of California, 1980), pp. 32, 92; and Sherri Grasmuck, "Immigration, Ethnic Stratification, and Native Working Class Descriptions: Comparisons of Documented and Undocumented Dominicans," *International Migration Review* 18 (Fall 1984): 692–713.

12. Grasmuck, 1984, p. 701.

13. Barry R. Chiswick, "The Effect of Americanization on the Earnings of Foreign-Born Men," *Journal of Political Economy* 86 (October 1978): 897–921; and Barry R. Chiswick, "Illegal Aliens in the U.S. Labor Market: Analysis of Occupational Attainment and Earnings," *International Migration Review* 18 (Fall 1984): 714–732.

14. Chiswick's coefficients estimated from the entire North and Houstoun (1976) sample for which the necessary variables were included were .0230 for years of education; .0238 for "experience" (age minus years of education minus 5); –.0005 for "experience" squared; .0644 for years since immigration; and –.0027 for years since immigration squared (Chiswick, 1984, p. 730). All of these estimates are statistically significant. The values of these coefficients imply that if the illegals in Sheldon Maram's sample (1980) had the same average years of education, "experience," and years since immigration as the legals, the wages received by the undocumented would rise by 31 percent. In comparison, the average wage for the legals in the sample was 40 percent above the average wage for the illegals. Furthermore, the large difference in months worked within the firm should also explain some of the difference.

15. Chiswick's coefficients estimated from the sample of foreign-born adult males in the 1970 *Census Public Use Samples of Basic Records* were .0574 for education; .0203 for "experience"; –.0003 for "experience" squared; .0150 for years since immigration; and –.0002 for years since immigration squared (Chiswick, 1978, table 2, column 5). All estimates were statistically significant, although in this case, estimates from a regression analysis using hourly wages are not available so coefficients from an equation in which annual earnings was the dependent variable are used. This equation did control for weeks worked, although not for hours per week. These estimates imply that if the legals in Maram's sample has values for education, "experience," and years since immigration equal to those values for the illegals, then the wages received by the legals would fall by 36 percent. In comparison, the average wage for the illegals in the sample was 28.5 percent below the average wage for the legals.

16. Orley Ashenfelter and Robert Smith, "Compliance with the Minimum Wage Law," *Journal of Political Economy* 87 (April 1979): 333–350.

17. Maram, 1980, p. 92; and North and Houstoun, 1976, pp. 129–130.

18. It is worth noting that exposure to the INS by other workers or acquaintances is probably a greater threat to the undocumented than exposure by employers, but the labor market implications of this danger from vindictive neighbors are not obvious. Resentment at taking jobs at below the minimum wage is at least one possible motivation.

19. Maram, 1980, p. 3.

20. Maram, 1980, p. 3.

21. Ashenfelter and Smith, 1979, p. 349.

22. This assumes that the penalty for violation is not a function of the difference between the wage that is actually paid and the minimum. If the violation is discovered, the first offenders usually must pay back all or part of the wages they would have had to pay. As Ashenfelter and Smith (1979) point out, such a payment *does not* constitute a penalty.

23. Maram's wage data are presented in discrete ranges. There are two categories for subminimum wages. The relative number of workers in those two ranges gives an indication of the underlying distribution of wages. If the wages of many workers fall into the lowest range, then the underlying distribution is weighted more toward the low end and the incentives to violate the law will grow. This is borne out by the data. The compliance ratio in the garment industry is .47, whereas it is .68 for the restaurant industry, but in the garment industry there are relatively more workers earning below $2.00 than in the restaurant industry. The same is true when legals and illegals are compared within each of the industries. Although the underlying distribution cannot be observed, the distortions caused by the presence of the minimum wage will not change this conclusion so long as it is assumed, as Ashenfelter and Smith do, that employers will have a greater incentive to comply for workers whose wages would be closest to the minimum.

24. Ashenfelter and Smith, 1979, p. 338.

25. Vernon M. Briggs, *Mexican Migration and the U.S. Labor Market* (Austin, Tex.: Center for the Study of Human Resources, University of Texas, 1975); and Walter Fogel, *Mexican Illegal Alien Workers in the United States* (Los Angeles, Cal.: Institute of Industrial Relations, University of California, 1978).

26. North and Houstoun, 1976.

27. This rate was derived by calculating an average of unionization rates by industry that was weighted by the distribution of employment by industry in the North-Houstoun sample. The unionization estimates were derived by Freeman and Medoff from *Current Population Survey* data for May 1973 and 1975. Richard Freeman and James L. Medoff, "New Estimates of Private Sector Unionism in the United States," *Industrial and Labor Relations Review* 32 (January 1979): 143–174.

28. Grasmuck, 1984.

29. NACLA,"Immigrant Workers in New York City," *Report on the Americas* 12 (November/December 1979); and Community Research Associates, 1981.

30. North and Houstoun, 1976, p. 132.

31. Community Research Associates, 1981, p. 228.

32. Maram, 1980, p. 103.

33. In the field survey of restaurants in New York, about one-sixth of the native-born owners interviewed stated that they rarely employed immigrants; one-tenth admitted that they required no documents, asked no questions, and did not want to know about the immigration status of their workers; and one-quarter said that they made some effort to check the status of their employees, although they did not require immigration documents—usually they just asked for a social security card. One said that he accepted an oral statement, and another said that he asked for a green card but would accept a lawyer's statement that the person was in the process of acquiring proper documents. Several said that they had found out that some of their workers were undocumented but usually only after a raid by the INS or because the Internal Revenue Service had informed them that an employee had used an invalid social security number or one that belonged to someone else. One-seventh insisted that they required "green cards" and swore that none of their employees were undocumented. Restaurant owners who were immigrants themselves were much more aware of the immigration status of their workers, admitting that some were indeed undocumented.

9

Conclusion

Despite the controversy generated by the potential for conflict and competition between recent immigrant groups and low-skilled natives, policy discussions have been based on a remarkably thin research foundation. Few studies have addressed this issue. And for the most part, research on subordinate groups, including the native born, has focused on how these groups compare to adult white males rather than how they relate to one another.

Although this book has been motivated by a specific immigration policy problem, a variety of demographic and technological developments makes the question that it addresses of more general interest. The postwar labor market pattern with its core of adult males, particularly white males, is breaking down. The most dramatic manifestation of this breakdown is the growth of the female labor force and the diversity within it: single women, heads of households, welfare recipients, and married women with children. The relative number of youth is now declining, but the proportion of minority youth—especially those in the inner cities—within that group is growing, and it is these young people who have experienced the greatest problems. Indeed, minorities of all ages are playing a more central role in the labor market as a result of immigration and internal population growth. In some cities, the white population has become the minority. The foreign-born population is also increasingly heterogeneous, as a result not only of greater ethnic diversity but also of the increasing proportion of refugees within the overall flow. Thus, labor market issues and controversies will increasingly relate to how these groups interact with one another rather than how they compare to white males.

For a study of the labor market impact of immigration, these interactions are the fundamental issues that need to be addressed.

Currently, the interactions are conceptualized in simple labor force dichotomies—skilled/unskilled or primary/secondary. Because immigrants do not uniquely occupy any of these categories, this structure imposes the assumption that the foreign born compete with fellow unskilled or secondary-sector workers. But skill or labor market segment classifications obscure central factors that shape and differentiate the labor market roles of the newcomers from those of the native born. Important differences between the two groups remain among workers of similar skill levels or the same occupation or industry. This disparity between immigrants and natives is rooted in the transitional nature of the immigration process, the particular conditions that bring various groups of native workers to the low-wage labor market, and the processes and institutions through which they find work and acquire skills. It is not that immigrants bring different skills, although in some cases they do, but that they are involved in a different *process* of labor market integration and mobility.

This comparative analysis of the roles of immigrants and natives has several implications for the ways in which we understand and study the labor market interaction among groups as well as the policies that we develop to confront immigration-related problems. First, as has been emphasized throughout this book, these factors do not necessarily eliminate competition between immigrants and natives, but they do reduce competition and open the possibility that immigrants and other low-wage or secondary-sector groups are complementary. This helps explain why the empirical evidence of labor market competition is so weak despite the apparent plausibility of the competition hypothesis.

Second, if the differences between immigrants and natives are based on processes that are inherently dynamic, then our understanding of the interactions between these groups will necessarily be incomplete, if not misleading, if we depend on static concepts such as skill level or current occupation for analysis of those differences. From this viewpoint, two unskilled dishwashers may have very different labor market roles. It is difficult to predict or analyze the consequences of reducing the availability of a particular group that provides a supply of dishwashers without some understanding of the factors that brought the members of that group to those jobs in the first place and of where they are likely to be employed in the future. Thus there will be important differences between changing the availability of teenage dishwashers, on the one hand, and immigrant dishwashers on the other.

Third, if the processes of labor market integration and mobility and the socioeconomic context that shapes those processes can differentiate low-skilled immigrants and natives, those processes can also create disparities among low-skilled native groups. Of the groups discussed in this book, both the quantitative and case study evidence suggests that immigrants more often compete with native women than with teenagers or black adult men. As a result, the effects of changes in immigration policy will vary among the native groups that would presumably benefit from immigration restriction. Although immigration restriction may strengthen the employment position of some groups, it may not help those groups for which the restriction was designed to benefit.

In examining the interaction between immigrants and native blacks, the book addresses the contrast between the continuing problems that confront blacks and the perception of immigrant success and economic mobility. Although this issue is not the main focus of the book, the analysis does shed some light on the discussion, particularly suggestions that blacks should pursue a strategy of self-help, entrepreneurship, and economic organization within their communities, a strategy that immigrants appear to have been able to use advantageously. The process of immigrant economic development based on small business and informal relationships is closely tied to the dynamics that are inherent in the act of immigration. For blacks, this is a process that has already run its course. For whatever reasons, they did not establish more small businesses when they as a group were engaged in the south-to-north migration; it is too late now to expect black economic development to follow the immigrant pattern. Piecemeal programs, such as those that provide financial assistance, cannot replace the complex advantages including access to cheap labor, training opportunities, and social networks that immigrants enjoy. And because blacks have tended to find success in large organizations and in the public sector, few successful blacks are now involved in developing a community-based economy.

Immigration Policy

The roots of the current immigration reform movement are complex and often contradictory. In addition to the potential impact on low-wage natives, pressures to change the immigration system arise from concern for national sovereignty, equity, justice, foreign policy, crime, culture, racism, and public expense, among others. Much of the anxiety is caused by the perception that the United States has simply lost control of its borders and is no longer able to regulate who can and cannot enter its labor market. Nevertheless, calls for change are not limited to measures designed to end illegal immigration but include suggestions for changing the criteria for legal immigration, the treatment of refugees, and many other aspects of the overall system.

The remainder of this chapter discusses the proposals and policy issues that relate directly to the particular analysis presented in this book. It is by no means a comprehensive discussion of immigration reform or an analysis of the specific provisions of the latest immigration reform—the Immigration Reform and Control Act of 1986. There are already several detailed discussions of immigration policy to which the reader unfamiliar with these issues and debates can refer.[1]

The Labor Market Impact

The evidence developed and presented in the previous chapters suggests that changes in the level of immigration have an uncertain and dispersed effect on the labor market position of low-skilled natives. Immigrants and many native groups play different labor market roles despite similar skill levels. These roles are not necessarily competitive and are sometimes complementary. And the empirical evidence does not suggest strong displacement or wage effects. This does not imply that the effect of an open border would have only minor effects. Conclusions from existing evidence only pertain to changes in the neighborhood of present immigration levels.

Furthermore, this research suggests that immigrants do compete with native women. This problem clearly needs more analysis. And the relationship between immigration and the employment problems of urban minority teenagers has received little attention. The analyses in Chapters 4 and 5 suggest why competition between immigrants and teenagers is not strong; nevertheless, the problems are serious enough to warrant further study.

There also may be reasons other than the labor market effects to increase control over entry. The present system rewards those who can manipulate the system and take advantage of its loopholes, creating an infrastructure of individuals and institutions that exist to carry out those manipulations. In fact, there is a clear incentive to break the law and jump the queue instead of waiting in line for the next legal slot in the quota. Whether or not we have "lost control of our borders," it does seem reasonable that entry should be based on equity or whatever criteria are established by the legislative process. How that control might be achieved depends on the importance placed on those factors relative to the costs of implementing the controls. Over the next decade, we will see whether employer sanctions are an effective means to regulate immigration. The impact of the sanctions will depend to a large extent on the vigor of the enforcement. Indeed, the restrictive potential of the previous immigration laws was never exploited.[2] Many of the problems that thwarted enforcement in the past have not been solved. Thus there are grounds for skepticism about the effectiveness of enforcement in the future.[3] Moreover, the arguments developed in this book and evidence from other studies suggest that if it is effective, the impact on the labor market problems of even unskilled natives will not be strong.

Family Reunification vs. Occupational Preferences

Since the 1965 amendments to the immigration laws, the legal immigration system has been primarily a family reunification system: If immediate family members of citizens are added to the quota ceiling, then almost 90 percent of the approximately 400,000 nonrefugees admitted annually are eligible because of familial relationships.[4] The 1986 immigration law will not reduce the central role of family reunification. There has been a continuing controversy over this focus. Economists have argued that the selection system should be based more on labor market considerations. According to this argument, more emphasis on labor certification would enhance productivity by increasing the skill level and amount of human capital that alien workers bring.[5] This approach would allow the immigration system to channel newcomers into skill areas where there are shortages and away from unskilled jobs, which presumably suffer from no supply shortage.[6] But the argument presented here calls into question the view that selecting immigrants on the basis of occupations would either reduce competition or improve the economy's productivity.

In considering this argument it is important to distinguish highly skilled and credentialed aliens with scarce technical knowledge from immigrants in lower skilled occupations for which there is a tight market. On the one hand, in many cases, immigrant PhDs and engineers do bring needed skills that cannot be quickly developed. Moreover, if they compete with natives, the possibility of more competition in the market for advanced degree holders hardly generates the urgency and concern that competition with the poor and unemployed does, although it might generate a faster political response. But even under the current system the highly skilled can often work in the United States either with a nonimmigrant visa or by taking advantage of the occupational preference slots that do exist.

On the other hand, what differentiates immigrants from natives is not so much their particular skill levels, but the process through which immigrants are incorporated into the labor market and through which they acquire skills. And familial networks play a central role in the process. Insofar as newcomers acquire eligibility to work through an organized process of occupational certification, it is likely that they will tend to be incorporated into the more organized and institutionalized sectors of the labor market. After all, it is these sectors that will be able to present their needs for labor most effectively and to make the appropriate arrangements to attract immigrant workers. But it is in precisely these sectors, in contrast to the informal sectors, that minorities, especially blacks, have made their most impressive labor market gains. Thus the family reunification-based immigration policy in effect strengthens the process of labor market integration that tends to differentiate immigrants of all skill levels from natives, and an occupational preference system might ultimately increase competition between immigrants and native minorities.[7]

Immigration-Related Labor Market Policy

Although the labor market impacts of immigration were certainly taken into account in the design of the 1986 immigration law, they were far from the only consideration. Foreign policy and other domestic political considerations played an important, and probably a dominant, role. Moreover, even if it were well established that immigration hurts the employment position of some groups, other groups would benefit from immigration either in the labor market or otherwise. Because it is unlikely that labor market objectives will be the primary determinant of the immigration system and because in any case the system of entry control will only be at best a blunt instrument for achieving labor market objectives, it is important that thinking and planning about immigration-related policy move beyond a focus on the national system of immigration regulation and include consideration of both the varied and the concentrated geographic impacts of a given level of immigration.

One policy area discussed in Chapter 8 concerns approaches to labor law enforcement that would prevent employers from using legal status to circumvent the objectives of that legislation. It was argued that insofar as legal status has an impact on the labor market in addition to the effect of increasing the numbers of workers, that impact resulted from the interaction between the immigrants and the institutions that regulate the labor market. For example, the presence of illegals was most likely to hamper the enforcement of the Fair Labor Standards Act when enforcement was based on complaint investigation. There is also evidence that the presence of undocumented workers thwarts the efforts of other workers to unionize.

Thus, as much as possible, minimum-wage enforcement should be based on random inspection in industries where violations are likely to occur rather than complaint follow-up. In a system of random inspection, the link between legal status and the effectiveness of enforcement would be cut. Moreover, attempts to use legal status to intimidate workers involved in union-organizing efforts should be punished as unfair labor practices; the Immigration and Naturalization Service (INS) should make a point of not following up complaints associated with organizing drives.

The effect on public budgets of the use of social services by immigrants has been debated almost as continuously as the labor market impact. Advocates of greater efforts to block use of tax-supported services by illegal immigrants argue that it will both reduce the incentives for illegal immigration and save public resources.[8] Although the argument that illegal immigrants threaten labor standards and wage levels is often based on the assumption that the undocumented are docile and easily intimidated, the conclusion that they drain the public coffers is based on their presumed sophistication and resourcefulness.[9]

To be sure, there are sophisticated as well as intimidated illegal immigrants. Nevertheless, there is a trade-off between labor market costs and social service costs. Insofar as immigrants have access to the benefits of social legislation, they need not be so dependent on the labor market for subsistence and will therefore not be so desperate for a job at any wage level. Efforts to block illegals from access to social services may therefore exacerbate negative labor market impacts.

Another approach to immigration-related labor market issues is to confront directly the problems of groups affected adversely by immigration. We have seen that this impact of immigration does vary significantly, even among the groups that fill low-level jobs. Although immigration restrictions may benefit some groups of native workers, the beneficiaries may not be the groups the policy was enacted to help.

But even if national employment and training policy were planned with these issues in mind, the burden of implementation would fall on the states and cities, primarily because immigration itself is so concentrated geographically.[10] Indeed, while immigration reform was stalled in Congress, many states and cities had already started to face this issue.[11]

Within the overall system of entry, states and cities with financial and technical assistance from Washington and with cooperation of the regional INS offices should develop local plans to confront immigration-related problems. These plans might include targeted enforcement designed, for example, to limit the employment of illegals in the more organized and institutionalized sectors of the economy that still hire low-skilled workers. Local and state governments could also design policy targeted to groups judged to be harmed by immigrants. And with the assistance of federally gathered data, local officials may be in the best position to understand the role and impact of the foreign born on local labor markets. Nevertheless, it is important to maintain a federal role, especially a federal financial and data-gathering role. In the end, immigration is a national issue, and its impact is ruled by national policy.

The implications of the immigration system as well as the policy development process reflect the national ambivalence about immigration. That ambivalence is rooted in the strength of the arguments on both sides of the controversy and in the ambiguity of the empirical evidence. If research demonstrated strong negative effects, which at least for the labor market it does not, then policy action might crystallize.

In any case, whatever the effects of the Immigration Reform and Control Act of 1986 and regardless of the long-run outcome of the immigration debate, serious labor market problems for unskilled natives will remain. These include the continuing drop in labor force participation among black males, the growth of poverty among female-headed families, and persistent high unemployment rates among urban minority teenagers and others. Current levels of immigration contribute to some of these problems; nevertheless, general immigration restriction is at best a blunt policy instrument. Moreover, the immigration debate should not distract us from more direct efforts to solve these labor market problems.

Notes

1. Michael Piore, *Birds of Passage: Migrant Labor and Industrial Societies* (New York, N.Y.: Cambridge University Press, 1979); Nathan Glazer, ed., *Clamor at the Gates: The New American Immigration* (San Francisco, Cal.: Institute for Contemporary Studies Press, 1985); Robert L. Bach, "Western Hemisphere Immigration to the United States: A Review of Selected Research Trends," Occasional Paper (Washington, D.C.: Center for Immigration Policy and Refugee Assistance, Georgetown University, 1985); Mary M. Kritz, ed., *U.S. Immigration and Refugee Policy: Global and Domestic Issues* (Lexington, Mass.: Lexington Books, 1983); U.S. Select Commission on Immigration Policy, *U.S. Immigration Policy and the National Interest*, Staff Report (Washington, D.C.: Commission on Immigration Policy, 1981); and Vernon M. Briggs, *Immigration Policy and the American Labor Force* (Baltimore, Md.: Johns Hopkins University Press, 1984).

2. The low budget and restricted manpower of the Immigration and Naturalization Service (INS) is one factor that hampers enforcement of the current system. The use of "voluntary departure," the positive weight given by the INS to "equity" developed during periods of illegal status, and the full range of legal rights and protections extended to illegals, whether they are justified or not, make vigorous enforcement difficult. For a discussion of the disparity between de jure and de facto immigration systems, see Briggs, 1984, chapter 5; Piore, 1979; and Edwin Harwood, "How Should We Enforce Immigration Law," in Glazer, 1985.

3. For an optimistic view on the effectiveness of sanctions, see U.S. General Accounting Office, *Illegal Aliens: Information on Selected Countries Employment Prohibition Laws*, Briefing Report (Washington, D.C.: General Accounting Office, October 1985). For a pessimistic view, Harwood, 1985.

4. Briggs, 1984, chapter 3.

5. Barry R. Chiswick, "Is the New Immigration More Unskilled than the Old," *Journal of Labor Economics* 4 (April 1986): 168–192.

6. Briggs, 1984, chapter 3.

7. Critics of the family reunification system also argue that it is unfair and "nepotistic" and that under the system it is almost impossible for aliens to immigrate who do not have family connections in the United States (Briggs, 1984). It is not obvious why an occupational preference system is more fair than a family preference system, but it does seem reasonable to give people without U.S. relatives a chance, especially because the preferences tend to restrict severely the immigration opportunities of individuals from countries that have not in the past sent newcomers to the United States. The proposal advocated by President Carter's Select Commission on Immigration and Refugee Policy that some slots be reserved for "seed" immigrants outside of the family and labor preferences does make sense in order to open immigration to aliens from a wider variety of countries.

8. David North, "Impact of Legal, Illegal, and Refugee Migration on the U.S. Social Service Programs," in Kritz, 1983.

9. For example, in an unpublished paper widely cited in the press, Donald Huddle, Arthur Corwin, and Gordon MacDonald argue that illegals engage in "introverted folk behavior" and that they "tend to keep to themselves in their own subcultures, and to manifest a natural distrust of officials, inspectors and political authorities. . . . " Yet in the same paper the authors suggest that each unemployed illegal receives "an average of $1800 [in unemployment benefits] over an 18-week period." Donald L. Huddle, Arthur F. Corwin, and Gordon J. MacDonald, "Illegal Immigration: Job Displacement and Social Costs" (Washington, D.C.: The Immigration Control Foundation, 1985), pp. 1, 10.

10. Briggs, 1984, chapter 8; and Michael Greenwood, "Regional Economic Aspects of Immigrant Location Patterns in the United States," in Kritz, 1983.

11. "Illegal Immigrants in U.S. are Problems Defying Easy Solution," *Wall Street Journal*, May 30, 1985, p. 1.

Appendix:
Selection of Interview Sample

A randomly selected list of 200 eating and drinking places was provided by the New York State Department of Labor (NYSDOL) from unemployment insurance records. The sample was stratified by employee size and borough. Restaurants were randomly selected from the list. In several cases, restaurants on the list were no longer in business. In other cases, no telephone listing could be found, because many restaurants do not do business under their corporate names. In these cases, if there was no restaurant at the address provided by the NYSDOL, the name was dropped from the sample. Restaurants with out-of-state addresses and airline caterers were also dropped. Most owners who were contracted were cooperative, but a few refused to be interviewed. Two owners agreed to be interviewed but refused to answer most of the questions.

Table A.1 presents employment data for the universe from which the sample was chosen, and Table A.2 presents the number of completed interviews from the NYSDOL sample by restaurant size class. In order to collect more information on chain restaurants and immigrant-owned restaurants, a second round of interviews was conducted with five of the former and thirteen of the latter restaurants. These were chosen from the telephone book.

Table A.3 presents the distribution of the restaurants surveyed according to the typology described in Chapter 1.

TABLE A.1
Restaurant Employment in Eating and Drinking Places (SIC 58), by Borough and Restaurant Size Class, New York City, 1979

| | Total | | Employment Size Class | | | | | |
| | | | 0-9 | | 10-99 | | 100+ | |
	Units	Employees	Units	Employees	Units	Employees	Units	Employees
Manhattan	5,145	68,977	3,473	12,805	1,600	39,596	72	16,576
Brooklyn	2,391	13,576	2,103	4,947	281	7,521	7	1,108
Queens	2,273	18,456	1,927	4,979	329	8,900	17	4,577
Total	9,809	101,009	7,503	22,731	2,210	56,017	96	22,261

Note: Size of firm data are for 1st Quarter, 1979.

Source: New York State Department of Labor.

TABLE A.2
Completed Interviews by Size Class from Sample Provided by New York State Department of Labor (NYSDOL)

| | Total | | Employment Size Class | | | | | | |
| | | | 0–9 | | 10–99 | | 100+ | |
	Interviews	NYSDOL Sample	Interviews	NYSDOL Sample	Interviews	NYSDOL Sample	Interviews	NYSDOL Sample
Manhattan	44	100	14	40	12	25	18	35
Brooklyn	15	40	4	20	6	13	5	7
Queens	11	60	2	23	7	20	2	17
Total	70	200	20	83	25	58	25	59

TABLE A.3
Distribution of Total New York Restaurants Surveyed, by Sector

Interviews	Total	Immigrant	Full-service	Intermediate	Fast-food
NYSDOL sample	60[a]	20	17	14	9
Other	21	13	2	3	3
Total	81	33	19	17	12

[a]Ten interviews were conducted with managers of bars, caterers, and industrial feeders. These establishments were not classified in the typology presented in Chapter 1.

About the Author

Thomas R. Bailey, an economist, is associate research scholar at Conservation of Human Resources, Columbia University. In addition to his work on immigration, he has served as a consultant on social policy issues and is the author of numerous articles on labor market problems and employment policy.

Index